FOOD ARTISANS
OF THE
OKANAGAN

YOUR GUIDE TO THE BEST LOCALLY CRAFTED FARE

JENNIFER COCKRALL-KING

TouchWood
Editions

TouchWood Editions
touchwoodeditions.com

The information in this book is true and complete to the best of the author's knowledge at
time of press. All recommendations are made without guarantee on the part of the author.
The author disclaims any liability in connection with the use of this information.

LIBRARY AND ARCHIVES CANADA CATALOGUING IN PUBLICATION
Cockrall-King, Jennifer, 1971–, author
Food artisans of the Okanagan : your guide to the best
locally crafted fare / Jennifer Cockrall-King.

Issued in print and electronic formats.
ISBN 978-1-77151-153-7

1. Local foods—British Columbia—Okanagan Valley (Region).
2. Food industry and trade—British Columbia. I. Title.

HD9000.5.C63 2016   338.1'9711'5   C2015-907636-6

Editor: Lana Okerlund
Proofreader: Claire Philipson
Designer: Pete Kohut
Maps: Eric Leinberger

Cover images:
Summerhill Landscape, courtesy of TourismKelowna.com and Summerhill Pyramid Winery,
by Brian Sprout; Artisan Baker, by Miquel Llonch/Stocksy United; Cheese on a Cutting Board,
by Liubov Burakova/Stocksy United; Yellow Plums, Holding Mushrooms, Cows in Field, and
Honeycomb, by Jennifer Cockrall-King. Pages ii–iii courtesy of TourismKelowna.com
and Tantalus Vineyards, by Brian Sprout.
All interior photos by Jennifer Cockrall-King unless otherwise noted.

We acknowledge the financial support of the Government of Canada through the Canada
Book Fund and the province of British Columbia through the Book Publishing Tax Credit.

Nous reconnaissons l'aide financière du gouvernement du Canada par l'entremise du Fonds du livre du
Canada et la province de la Colombie-Britannique par le Crédit d'impôt pour l'édition de livres.

This book was produced using FSC®-certified, acid-free papers,
processed chlorine free, and printed with soya-based inks.

20 19 18 17 16   1 2 3 4 5

PRINTED IN CHINA

For my husband, Michael King, who instinctively knew back in 2005 that we needed to be here. Honey, you were so right.

This book is also for all the food artisans of the Okanagan and Similkameen. The food culture of our region is being built by your daily labours and your belief in quality culinary craft. With every bite and sip, we thank you.

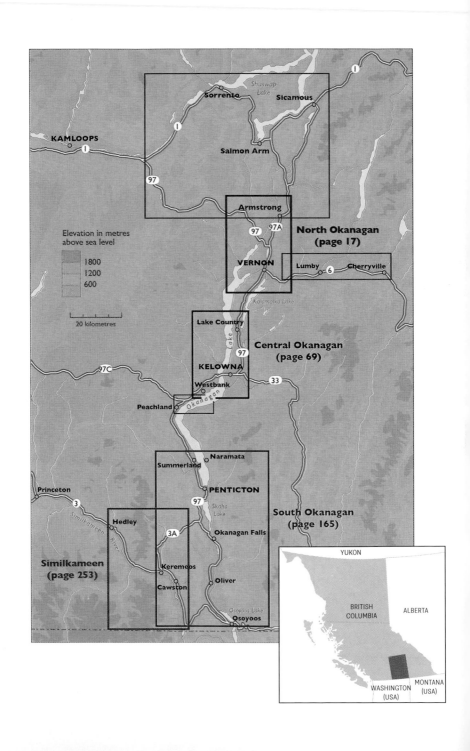

Elevation in metres
above sea level

1800
1200
600

20 kilometres

KAMLOOPS

Sorrento

Shuswap Lake

Sicamous

Salmon Arm

Armstrong

North Okanagan
(page 17)

VERNON

Lumby

Cherryville

Kalamalka Lake

Lake Country

Central Okanagan
(page 69)

KELOWNA

97C

Westbank

Okanagan Lake

33

Peachland

Naramata

Summerland

PENTICTON

Skaha Lake

South Okanagan
(page 165)

Princeton

Hedley

3A

Okanagan Falls

Similkameen River

Similkameen
(page 253)

Keremeos

Oliver

Cawston

Osoyoos Lake

Osoyoos

YUKON

BRITISH
COLUMBIA

ALBERTA

WASHINGTON
(USA)

MONTANA
(USA)

CONTENTS

INTRODUCTION

AS A FOOD WRITER, I travel to many of the world's culinary hot spots and trendy wine regions both for work and for pleasure. There's no doubt, they all have their charms, and there are invariably a few highlights. So why am I always so happy to return home to the Okanagan Valley?

For me, the Okanagan just has the complete package: lakes, mountains, vineyards, farms, and lots of breathing room within a closely knit culinary family. Chefs in the valley really do hang out with one another and support each other's restaurants and initiatives. Winemakers share space and equipment collegially. Farmers, brewers, bakers, and butchers gather at each other's potlucks and picnics. The community is not so big that you develop a headache trying to decide where to go for a bite to eat. And the region is not so small that you want for newness and excitement. And the food? To be blunt, whether it's in my kitchen, in a restaurant, at a roadside fruit stand, or at any one of the region's crazy-good farmers' markets, there's nowhere else I'd rather be.

Unlike some lucky Western Canadians, I didn't really get to know the Okanagan until I was in my mid-20s. In my childhood, our family did the "three kids and the dog in the back of the Ford Station Wagon" trek from Edmonton. After our 12-hour trip, the lake was too cold for my parents' liking, so it was our one and only visit. I was three years old at the time, so my memory of it is understandably fuzzy. I do, however, randomly recall the excitement of minigolf.

I returned to the Okanagan two decades later as an emerging food writer. In 2000, the buzz was starting to build in Kelowna. The steady, patient work of Okanagan wine pioneers and a few dedicated chefs was starting to pay off. The leap in ideology from making bulk wines to adopting the VQA (Vintners Quality Alliance) quality and origin standards triggered a shift in the culinary scene as well, which raised the bar for both chefs and farmers alike.

When I attended a major Canadian culinary conference in Kelowna in 2000, I will never forget my awe at seeing photo-perfect orchards, heavy with apples and pears. I returned again the following year on a tour hosted by Wines of British Columbia, then known as the British Columbia Wine Institute. In 2005, my husband, Mike, and I bought a house in Naramata. We didn't know it, but we had arrived just in time to watch the Okanagan wine scene explode with assertive new wineries and to enjoy Okanagan chefs unleashing their ambitions in this exciting new culinary landscape.

A few key chefs and their restaurants led the way. Already in the 1990s there was something uniquely Okanagan about the food that Kelowna-born chef Grant de Montreuil was cooking at his own De Montreuil restaurant. (He would also leave his mark on menus at the Hotel Eldorado, the Naramata Heritage Inn & Spa, Summerhill Pyramid Winery, and the Cove Lakeside Resort in West Kelowna.) Chefs Rod Butters and Audrey Surrao (who now own and operate RauDZ Regional

Table and Micro Bar Bites) opened Fresco in downtown Kelowna in 2001 and launched the farm-to-table frenzy in the valley. Butters had chef Mark Filatow, now at the helm of his own Waterfront Wines, in Fresco's opening brigade. Chef Bernard Casavant, already a superstar and a founding member of FarmFolk CityFolk, arrived from the West Coast and Whistler in 2006 to bring Burrowing Owl Estate Winery's Sonora Room onto the map in Osoyoos. These and other chefs—many of whom are covered in this book—spent incredible amounts of time and energy scouring the region for top-notch products. They sought out the farmers and orchardists who had already decided that the future of Okanagan cuisine depended on good land stewardship and quality, flavourful, healthy food. There was a palpable energy among the chefs, vintners, farmers, and appreciative diners.

A second wave of ambitious young chefs and food artisans arrived around 2005-6. They were drawn from their metropolitan locations by the quality of the products in the Okanagan—which was better than what they could access in the big cities—and by the fact that they could afford to live in the communities where they worked. They came from the country's top restaurant kitchens and took a risk on the Okanagan's future. I'm thinking of chef and now winemaker Heidi Noble of JoieFarm Winery (who in 2015 reopened her tasting room to include a menu from her wood-fired oven). I'm thinking of Cameron Smith and Dana Ewart, chef-owners of Joy Road Catering, who trained under Normand Laprise of Toqué! in Montreal and Jamie Kennedy in Toronto and brought *al fresco cuisine du terroir* to its potential at their incredible God's Mountain dinners above Skaha Lake. And Rhys Pender and Alishan Driediger, who opened Okanagan Grocery Artisan Breads in Kelowna (they now make wine at their Little Farm Winery in Cawston). These food artisans saw the potential and were willing to put in an incredible amount of work to realize their dreams, all the while feeding a food culture that would soon be the envy of the rest of Canada.

The most recent major development has been in the craft beer, cider, and spirits community. In March 2014, licensing rules for small and craft breweries, cideries, and distilleries in BC changed for the better. The changes took years of patient advocacy work from the likes of Tony and Tyler Dyck, the father-son team behind western Canada's pioneering Okanagan Spirits, on behalf of all craft alcohol producers in BC, but we're oh so glad those changes happened. Old rules about zoning and crippling markup were updated. Policies were put in place that have been a boon not only for the value-added booze producers, but just as importantly for the farmers and orchardists who grow the primary products that go into BC craft gin, vodka, whisky, cider, and beer.

This is why we're seeing a sudden rush of new producers in this market. They can now build tasting rooms and operate on-farm, like BX Press on the Dobernigg family orchard in Vernon, or in busy urban centres, like Old Order Distilling in downtown Penticton, one street off Main. As long as craft producers use 100 percent BC-grown grain, malt, or fruit, they can sell direct to consumers without any markup (which was previously as high as 167 percent per bottle). Equally important, these small-business owners can continue to invest in quality because they now have enough critical mass to play a part in the valley's culinary tourism routes. The craft distillery, beer, and cider boom might just be enough to draw people back onto small farms, because it now looks viable for the next generation to make a living and a life on-farm growing raw ingredients like barley, hops, grains, and botanicals. (I'll drink to that!)

Let's just say we've now got some momentum happening, but it is due to the patience and work of every farmer, orchardist, baker, brewer, distiller, chef, and winemaker who had a long-term vision that *only the best* products, dining experiences, and wine from the region would do.

This book is an attempt to capture the people, the passion, and the momentum of the Okanagan's culinary scene, even if it is changing day to day. Maybe it's because I didn't grow up in the valley, but after 10 years

here, I still feel like I am discovering new places and new people who are doing the most exciting things. This book is all about those discoveries. So please join me and we'll head off together to meet the Food Artisans of the Okanagan.

HOW THIS BOOK IS ORGANIZED

When friends and family announce they are coming to the Okanagan, I remind them that they're talking about a 20,000-square-kilometre (7,700-square-mile) area. In other words, the Okanagan covers a lot of ground, both physically and from a foodshed perspective. There are mountains, lakes, and streams for wild foods like mushrooms, watercress, trout, and salmon. The open expanses of the north allow grain and dairy farming, livestock, and poultry. The rolling hills that flow south from the Central Okanagan are perfect for fruit orchards and vineyards. The enormous glacial Lake Penticton, which formed about 12,000 years ago and drained about 8,000 years ago, left behind incredible silt and loam for vegetable and berry farming in flat spots in Kelowna and in the claybanks and benchlands from Naramata to Okanagan Falls. Then there's the scorching desert of the South Okanagan and Similkameen, where fanatical farmers grow the most flavour-intense peppers, tomatoes, eggplants, melons, and cantaloupes I've ever tasted.

The differing geographies, climates, histories, and cultural quirks and vibes of the North, Central, and South Okanagan led me to organize the food artisans and businesses featured in this book geographically first, and then by category. The distinctiveness of each area is really one of the unexpected pleasures of living out here. I will never stop marvelling at the nuances I continue to discover between Naramata and Summerland, or Summerland and Peachland, let alone Armstrong and Osoyoos. Never before have I experienced a place where the geography and even microclimates dictate the pace of life as they do here.

From the start, I knew I also needed to include the Similkameen, which includes Cawston, "Organic Capital of Canada," and Keremeos, "Fruit Stand Capital of Canada." The Similkameen Valley has its own character, its own geography, its own history, and its own winery region. It's about one-twentieth the size of the Okanagan, but it's an important contributor to the culinary and wine culture of the region. Since fruits, grapes, wines, chefs, locals, and tourists flow so freely between the Okanagan and the Similkameen, it just made sense to include my favourite food artisans from there as well.

Where are the wineries in this book, you ask? The long answer is that while winemakers are culinary artisans, there are already several excellent books about them. In particular, *John Schreiner's Okanagan Wine Tour Guide*, now in its fifth edition, does an excellent job of profiling winemakers and keeping abreast of the ever-changing wine scene in the region. *Food Artisans of the Okanagan* shines the spotlight on the other side of our amazing culinary region: the market gardeners, the chocolatiers, the vinegar makers, and the bakers who don't seem to get as much food media coverage as they should. I also include cidermakers, distillers, craft brewers, and meadmakers who, though a fairly small group at the moment, are rapidly growing in numbers, so their addition gives a special sparkle to this book. I was wedging new paragraphs into the pages here up until press time.

ABOUT OKANAGAN TERROIR

The word *terroir* gets bandied around a lot these days in various food and wine regions, and I use it in this book as well. Terroir is a French wine term that encompasses the physical characteristics of a place—soil, climate, location, exposure, altitude, etc.—and the foods that spring from that place and its culinary traditions, practices, and attitudes. Certainly, wine drinkers can taste how Riesling grapes grown on the Naramata Bench have different characteristics and flavours than Riesling grapes grown in Alsace, but there are also differences from vineyard to vineyard, winemaker to winemaker. In food, as in drink, terroir speaks to why a

muskmelon grown in a field in Oliver and picked at its peak of fragrance and flavour will have different taste characteristics than a muskmelon grown by a different farmer, using different growing techniques, on a different piece of land.

Terroir is about distinctiveness, which is celebrated and even encouraged in the world of craft culinary artisans. It's what sets craft products apart from large-scale, and most certainly industrial-scale, products. Honey gathered in the North Okanagan, with its clover and fruit-blossom sweetness, will be deliciously different from honey gathered in the south, where camphorous desert plants or lavender notes are present. Some years the carrots in the Okanagan are extraordinarily carrot-y. (This happened about four years ago. I don't know why. All I know is that I bought and enjoyed more carrots that summer than I ever had before.) Some years the peaches have a fragrance and texture that will make you weep; other years the cherries or the apricots shine through. Some years the salmon run is ridiculously abundant; other years it's worrisome.

Terroir also touches on how the cultural mosaic of people in the region use the primary products. Why did the Okanagan nations work for decades to renaturalize the damaged and dammed waterways that almost destroyed the natural sockeye run that had fed their families for thousands of years? Why did German-born Frank Deiter buy a still to make fruit brandies in Vernon that became Okanagan Spirits? Why can you get incredible hot, homemade samosas with freshly dug potatoes and freshly hulled green peas to go at many of the fruit stands in Oliver and Osoyoos? Cultural traditions, whether indigenous or part of the multicultural makeup of the valley, come to bear on why we grow certain foods and why we turn those ingredients into smoked fish, jams and jellies, or eaux-de-vie. We're on the cusp of a coherent culinary distinctiveness with our Okanagan terroir. For me, terroir has a lot to do with people—the people we meet in *Food Artisans of the Okanagan*.

ABOUT ORGANICS

Knowing that sustainable, non-environmentally harmful, and non-toxic farming practices go into making, growing, and raising my food is important to me. Assuring that the livestock that becomes a pork chop, drumstick, or rib eye are being raised ethically and as naturally as possible is the least I can do as a meat eater. And I feel good knowing that my small purchasing choices can support a type of agriculture that attempts to pay a living wage to the farmers and labourers who break their backs for good, healthy, high-quality food.

As consumers, we rarely have time to research thoroughly. Luckily, we have a set of checks and regulations that govern the use of the term that encompasses these principles. In Canada, to be *certified organic* is to be in line with these environmental, social, ethical, and food-quality values. There's a cost to the farmer or producer for this certification because it involves oversight, audits, and additional administration. However, when you buy directly from the farmer or rancher, the extra cost is barely noticeable.

If a farmer uses the term "organic," ask to see the certification credentials. You're either certified organic or you're not. Period. In BC, look for a logo of a green checkmark inside a gold rectangular frame; across Canada, there is a round logo that says "Canada Organic · Biologique Canada" with a red maple leaf rising over a green field.

You'll notice that some of the farms I write about are certified organic and some are not. Ideally all the people in this book would go the extra mile to be certified organic. However, it's not my job to tell people how to do their job. My job is to shine a light on excellent products and the people who take an artisanal approach to making, growing, or raising food in my Okanagan foodshed. If you do get to know your farmer, and she or he tells you they are "organic in practice" and just don't have the money to pay for certification, I encourage you to have a conversation with them about how much more money it would cost you, the consumer, and whether you'd be willing to pay. Otherwise, the term is wide-open to abuse and deceptive labelling.

I feel comfortable that the people I write about in these pages, and from whom I buy the food I put on my table for my friends and family, are good land and animal stewards. And I like to think that a book like this can encourage people that their purchasing power, even at an individual scale, is part of a virtuous circle that leads to a living wage for farmers and keeps the supply of quality food flowing.

ABOUT THE MEASUREMENTS USED IN THE PROFILES

I know, we're metric in Canada. Normally I'm uncompromising on that subject—except when it comes to food. Farmers talk about the size of their farms in acres, even farmers in their 20s. Rather than not accurately quote them, I have left acres as acres because no one in farming really thinks in hectares.

ABOUT CHEFS

This won't be news to anyone familiar with professional cooking and the restaurant business, but chefs move around. A lot. I list and mention their current places of employment at the time of press, but with the knowledge—or even expectation—that some will take on new posts and challenges.

That said, I have noticed that once a chef works in the Okanagan, with all of the amazing raw ingredients and outstanding wines, craft beers, spirits, and ciders, they really only shuffle around within the valley. Some move from the south to the north, or from the north to the central valley, but very few leave the region.

In the 10 years I've been here, in fact, there's been a net influx of chefs from cities like Calgary, Vancouver, Toronto, and Edmonton, and they delight in buying direct from farmers, market gardeners, and orchardists. Though this is definitely more work than placing one large order with a big foodservice warehouse and delivery company, Okanagan chefs value the relationships and the connection to the seasons here that they can't have in any other place.

WHAT IS A FOOD ARTISAN AND HOW DID I CHOOSE WHOM TO INCLUDE IN THIS BOOK?

What is a food artisan? I thought a lot about this question, even as I was already interviewing and writing about the people in this book. I didn't start out with established "food artisan" criteria first and then include only people that fit the mould. Instead, I trusted my gut on this one—and lest you think this is a terrible pun, it's not. I very literally trusted my taste buds. I put myself on the spot and listed the people who sprang to mind when I simply thought of the best-tasting, most interesting, and most memorable products, meals, and ingredients from the Okanagan. The food that each producer was involved with growing, fishing, foraging, making, baking, brewing, or cooking had to have incredible, memorable flavour. I also asked each food artisan very pointed questions about their purpose and how they worked. Then I looked at their involvement in creating the amazing culinary community in the region, even if they didn't have the time and energy in their busy days to think about how they were playing a part. Yes, the choices I make in this book are subjective. They reflect my palate and my preferences. The artisans included in this book are of my choosing alone, so they reflect my tastes and network.

This leads me to my last point: this is not the definitive list of all the food artisans at work building our thriving culinary community. This is my snapshot of where the Okanagan is at a point in time. I have done my best to interview and include every excellent culinary artisan in the area. Success breeds more success. Undoubtedly, by the time this book is in print, there will be new artisan food products and producers I'll want to include. I imagine that new chefs, new culinary entrepreneurs, and a new crop of farmers are already making plans to launch new ventures. I also have no doubt that I'll have missed a great food artisan or two, so if you feel that a person or product deserves to be in a future edition, please let me know via email, Twitter, or the book's Facebook page or blog (see page 311 for contact details).

NORTH OKANAGAN

- ARMSTRONG
- CHERRYVILLE
- COLDSTREAM
- LUMBY
- VERNON

NORTH OKANAGAN

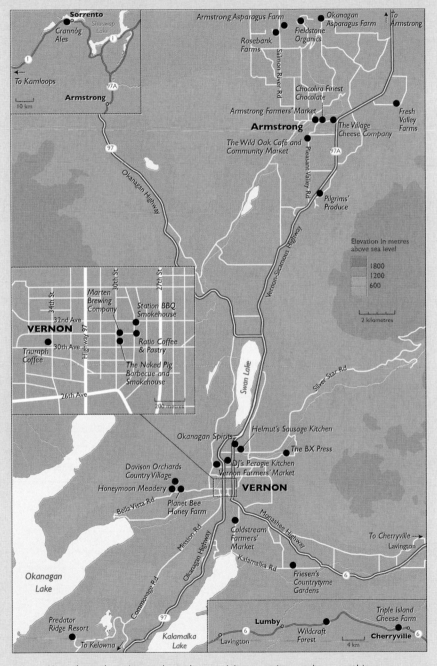

Sorrento

Crannóg
Ales

Shuswap
Lake

To Kamloops

10 km

Armstrong

Armstrong Asparagus Farm

Okanagan
Asparagus Farm

To
Armstrong

Fieldstone
Organics

Rosebank
Farms

Salmon River Rd

Chocoliro Finest
Chocolate

Armstrong Farmers' Market

Armstrong

The Village
Cheese Company

Fresh
Valley
Farms

The Wild Oak Café and
Community Market

Pleasant Valley Rd

97A

Pilgrims'
Produce

Okanagan Highway

Vernon-Silverus Highway

Elevation in metres
above sea level

1800

1200

600

2 kilometres

30th St

Marten
Brewing
Company

27th St

Station BBQ
Smokehouse

34th St

32nd Ave

Highway 97

VERNON

30th Ave

Ratio Coffee
& Pastry

Triumph
Coffee

The Naked Pig
Barbecue and
Smokehouse

26th Ave

200 metres

Swan Lake

Silver Star Rd

Helmut's Sausage Kitchen

Okanagan Spirits

The BX Press

Davison Orchards
Country Village

DJ's Perogie Kitchen
Vernon Farmers' Market

Honeymoon Meadery

VERNON

Bella Vista Rd

Planet Bee
Honey Farm

Mission Rd

Okanagan Highway

Monashee Highway

To Cherryville

Coldstream
Farmers'
Market

Lavington

Kalamalka Rd

Commonage Rd

Okanagan
Lake

97

Friesen's
Countrytyme
Gardens

6

Predator
Ridge Resort

Kalamalka
Lake

To Kelowna

Lumby

6

Wildcraft
Forest

4 km

Triple Island
Cheese Farm

Cherryville

6

Lavington

Note that only artisans who welcome visitors on site are shown on this map.

THE NORTH OKANAGAN IS A wide, fertile valley that begins at the north end of Okanagan Lake and extends up through orchards, farmland, meadows, and ranches. It's also the traditional land of Okanagan peoples who have hunted deer and rabbit, caught fish, and foraged here for as many generations as we can count.

With more annual precipitation than elsewhere in the Okanagan-Similkameen, 151 frost-free days, and fertile land, the North Okanagan is remarkable in its agricultural diversity. From grains to fruits, dairies to distilleries, the North Okanagan is always a revelation. Dutch and German influences explain the abundance of Gouda cheese, smoked meats, sausages, and weighty, grainy breads. Organic and sustainable farming took root in the late 1960s and 1970s in the North Okanagan, and now a new generation of farmers is making its mark with ambitious market gardens, agritourism operations, and Community Supported Agriculture (CSA) programs offering sustainable, local meat, poultry, eggs, fruits, and vegetables.

The area around Armstrong comprised low-lying swamps and willows when settlers arrived around 1866. They drained the swampland around the turn of the 20th century to expose rich soil that resulted in Armstrong's early nickname of "Celery City." While celery isn't the signature crop any-more, asparagus and grain growers, dairy farms, orchards, and market gardens create a mix of homegrown food within this artsy, cozy community.

Vernon, is known for its 140-plus-vendor farmers' market on Mondays and Thursdays, plus its Friday-night street market down the main com-mercial avenue in the summer. Vernon is also the home of the province's craft distilling movement. In 2015, the pioneering Okanagan Spirits opened its new $3 million tasting lounge the week after it won a pile of medals, including World Class Distillery and Distillery of the Year, at the World Spirits Awards. Hot on the heels of distilling, the energy around the craft beer and craft cider scene is palpable in the north.

Lumby and Cherryville lie to the east of Vernon, where farms and orchards snug up to the forests and foothills of the Monashee Mountains.

PLANET BEE HONEY FARM

5011 Bella Vista Road, Vernon | 250-542-8088 | planetbee.com

Beekeeper ED NOWEK runs around 300 to 400 hives in the Vernon area, depending on the year. Yes, that many hives produce a lot of honey, but Planet Bee is a major business and the store is open 365 days a year selling honey and other bee products. There's a honey tasting bar in-store where you can sample various local, national, and international honeys—though I always walk out with a little jar of Okanagan terroir produced by Nowek's bees. I'm partial to the clear, syrupy Fireweed Blossom honey as well as the multifloral Okanagan Wildflower.

There can literally be busloads of tour groups at Planet Bee on any given day (Christmas and New Year's Day included) buying up its apitherapy products: pollen, propolis, beeswax, and royal jelly in creams, soaps, shampoos, conditioners, and body lotions, including its own line of "Let it Bee" body care products. Planet Bee is also home to the Honeymoon Meadery, which has a tasting room on-site as well (see page 56).

Ed Nowek

Igor and Irma Ruffa

BELLA STELLA CHEESE

250-547-6305 | bellastellacheese.com

IGOR RUFFA was surrounded by traditional cheesemaking "with copper pots over a fire" during his boyhood summers in the Swiss-Italian Alps. At 19, he started to make his own cheese as a hobby, but went to work for Swisscom, one of the country's major telecommunications providers. His heart, however, remained with agriculture and cheesemaking.

Igor's wife, IRMA, grew up in Germany and also fancied the cheese-making life. After extensive cheesemaking training in Switzerland in 2004, Igor and Irma started working together as "mountain farmers" in the Swiss-Italian Alps, raising goats and making cheese. However, land and even small stone sheds for cheesemaking were out of their price range.

Now they make incredible, fresh, mild-tasting artisan cheeses in Lumby. Igor picks up milk twice a week from a neighbouring certified organic dairy farm, from which he makes four classic cheeses from the Swiss Ticino region in 300-litre (80-gallon) batches with cheesemaking equipment imported from Europe. Bella Stella's Formaggino is a fresh, spreadable cheese with a slightly acidic bite that comes in original (plain), herbes de Provence, and garden herb. The Formagella is a soft, creamy (sticky) cheese with a delicate white bloomy rind that's aged at least three weeks in Bella Stella's climate-controlled cooler. Montagna is a butter-coloured, mild-flavoured, semi-soft cheese with a brined rind that is aged three to four months. The Ricotta is an incredibly delicate, soft, snowy-white fresh cheese that tastes of fresh milk. Cut it into small wedges and drizzle with local honey and walnuts or hazelnuts. They've recently added a yogurt, a Quark (Swiss-style fresh, creamy cheese), and a seasonal Raclette.

Bella Stella doesn't have a farm-gate retail scenario, but you can find their certified organic cheeses in retail locations in Lumby, Armstrong, Vernon, and Kelowna. Irma also sells at farmers' markets in Coldstream, Armstrong, Salmon Arm, and Vernon; check their website for details or email Igor at bellastellacheese@gmail.com.

TERROIR CHEESE

3475 Smith Drive, Armstrong | 250-550-9597 | terroircheese.ca

Intensity and enthusiasm seem to run in LEN MARRIOTT's veins. For a mid-life career change, he went to France to take cheesemaking courses—in French, no less—and returned to make cheese in the North Okanagan. "BC has the best milk in Canada," he tells me. "And Canada has the best milk in the world." Now *that's* the kind of enthusiasm you want in an artisan cheesemaker.

Given his cheesemaking training in France, it's no accident that Marriott named his artisanal cheese company Terroir after that all-encompassing French term for how microclimate, weather, soil, method of production, and ingredients swirl together to produce a distinctive flavour specific to *that* product in *that* region. In Marriott's case, his cheeses are made from the milk of his own Montbéliarde-Holstein herd, which he keeps on a farm just north of Vernon—true field-to-fork control, down to the tiniest measure. Because his cows eat only grass and hay from his farm and surrounding fields, even their digestive micro-organisms have terroir. He also supplies his own GMO-free, organic feed for his cows. For the curd nerd, his website lists the exacting conditions under which he produces his cheeses.

Marriott's cheeses have analogues with European styles, but since the terroir is different, he gives them their own names. Jurassic is a creamy, pressed, non-cooked cheese that is aged 45 days on spruce boards and has a distinctive centre line of ash running through it. His French Gruyère is a straw-coloured, hard-cooked cheese with a brushed rind; it's excellent to eat as is or melted, like on a French onion soup or in fondue. Mt. Ida, a soft, unaged cheese (like a Brie), is made with pasteurized milk because of local laws. This creamy cheese screams out for pears or apple slices. His raw-milk Continental Blue is Stilton-style. And the Artisan Jarlsberg is a hard eating or melting cheese with faint aromas of hazelnuts. Check Terroir Cheese's website for farmers' market attendance and other retail locations.

Len Marriott

Kees Tuijtel

TRIPLE ISLAND CHEESE FARM

1519 Highway 6, Cherryville | 250-547-6125

The cost of farmland in Holland caused the Tuijtel family to look for a place in Canada in 2001. They found an old feedlot on Highway 6 between Lumby and Cherryville and converted it into a 74-acre family-run dairy farm and cheesemaking operation. JOHAN TUIJTEL tends the dairy herd while his son, KEES TUIJTEL, makes the cheese in the small farm-gate cheese shop right on the highway. It takes 750 litres (200 gallons) of whole milk to produce 75 kilograms (165 pounds) of cheese.

Although Triple Island seems to be in the middle of nowhere, a steady flow of customers drop in for its farmstead Maasdammer (like a Swiss Emmental, except without the holes) made from a recipe that dates back four generations, and Kees's various mild, medium, aged, smoked, and flavoured Goudas. These creamy, excellent raw-milk cheeses can also be purchased at the Vernon Farmers' Market and Kelowna Farmers' and Crafters' Market, as well as a few select specialty grocery stores in the North and Central Okanagan.

THE VILLAGE CHEESE COMPANY

3475 Smith Drive, Armstrong | 250-546-8651 | villagecheese.com

It's fitting that a cheese shop should be a major landmark and gathering place—look for the clock tower—in Armstrong, a town with a century-old history of making cheese. Locals gather at the Village Cheese Company café for coffee and borscht and to buy cheese, which is made with fresh, local whole milk and has no additives like milk by-products or artificial preservatives. The line of cheese is extensive, but a few stand-outs include the organic raw-milk cheddars and organic cow feta, the Amber Ale Ripened Soft Cheese, the Smokehouse Cheddar, and the 11-year Aged Cheddar.

Everything is done in-house, from the cheesemaking to the smoking to the packaging. NORM BESNER is the head cheesemaker, and you can watch him and his crew at work through the large windows between the cheese shop and the retail café.

Armstrong Cheese originated in Armstrong, BC, in 1902. The brand was bought out by Dairyworld in 1997, which was in turn acquired by Saputo, a multinational corporation, in 2001. Armstrong Cheese is now connected to the town of Armstrong only in name.

The Village Cheese Company, Armstrong

Jolanda and Peter Rotzetter

CHOCOLIRO FINEST CHOCOLATE

3495 Pleasant Valley Road, Armstrong | 250-546-2886 | chocoliro.ca

As far as I'm concerned, a town of two people needs at least one good chocolate shop. I was pleased to discover Chocoliro, a small, tidy shop with hand-poured chocolates, along Armstrong's main thoroughfare, and clearly I'm not the only one. This place has a loyal following, and for good reason.

PETER AND JOLANDA ROTZETTER immigrated to Armstrong from Muenchenbuchsee, Switzerland, in 2010 because the area appealed to them with its wide-open fields, lakes, and nearby mountains. "I also like wine," adds Peter cheerily. They opened Chocoliro later that fall, and the shop has been a going concern ever since. Peter says that the obvious choice of community would have been a larger centre like Kelowna, but Armstrong has embraced Chocoliro, and business has been good.

Rather than importing a brand like Lindt that is available everywhere, the Rotzetters import Carma chocolate from Zurich, some of which is UTZ-certified, the largest program for sustainable farming of coffee and cocoa in the world. UTZ certification covers criteria such as sustainable farm management, ethical working conditions, environmentally responsible production techniques, and quality control of the drying and fermenting of cocoa beans.

Jolanda is the chocolatemaker, painting and pouring the chocolate into moulds and creating filled chocolates that change regularly. Peter minds the tidy shop, a far cry from his former career in banking. Chocoliro's 70 percent dark chocolate with pepper is my personal choice, but given that Armstrong is dairy and cow country, Peter says that their "fancy chocolates," especially the big brown and white cows, are local best-sellers.

RATIO COFFEE & PASTRY

3101 29th Street, Vernon | 250-545-9800 | ratiocoffee.ca

ANDREW MCWILLIAM grew up on Vancouver Island and has become the driving force behind third-wave coffee in Vernon. He had his artisan coffee conversion moment over a decade ago at Drumroaster Coffee in Cobble Hill on Vancouver Island. "Then I became that crazy coffee-hobby enthusiast guy for about 10 years afterwards," he laughs.

McWilliam's career in youth work brought him to Vernon in 2009, but he just couldn't find a coffee culture here that could support his habit. He imported beans from Drumroaster and made coffee at his home for friends and family. His brother arrived in Vernon in 2012, and together they started a pop-up coffee stand at the Vernon Farmers' Market, doing "pour-over" coffees (not espresso extraction) and offering a small home delivery service for good beans. They called their pop-up Grey Canal Coffee, after the Grey Canal irrigation system that brought water to the farmlands and orchards of Vernon at the turn of the 20th century. In 2014, McWilliam partnered with Robin and Mat Hewitt to open Triumph Coffee (see page 35). The partnership ended shortly after Triumph opened, but that freed up McWilliam to partner with pastry chef LAURIE KNUEVER to bring Ratio Coffee & Pastry to life.

In addition to Ratio, McWilliam's growing Coffee Club allows him to source beans from expert roasters across Canada and curate his club subscribers' monthly bean delivery as Vernon's only coffee bean valet. Join the club at andrewcoffee.ca.

Laurie Knuever and Andrew McWilliam

Third-wave coffee is most easily recognized by the lovely latte art your barista makes just before she hands you your custom order. At a deeper level, however, it's a movement that treats coffee beans as an artisanal product and celebrates craft in all aspects of the final brewed or espresso-extracted coffee. Relationships matter in third-wave coffee: between growers and bean brokers, between roasters and coffee shop owners, and between baristas and customers. There's an appreciation for the differences that can be traced to the farm on which the beans were grown and in what conditions. (In very broad terms, these factors express themselves in the acidity and flavour profiles of the coffee.) Brewing methods also play a large role in third-wave coffee conversation, and high-tech and low-tech geekery is a source of great enjoyment for coffee aficionados.

What I like is that, with the increased quality of the coffee bean and the artisan approach to roasting, there's also an awareness that the farmer who grows the beans in an environmentally sustainable way should be paid fairly. It's not just about latte art after all.

Robin Hewitt

TRIUMPH COFFEE

3401 A 30th Avenue, Vernon | 778-475-1288 | triumphcoffee.ca

ROBIN HEWITT moved to Vernon around 2009 with her husband Mat and their young family. Having previously lived in Victoria and Montreal, and as a young mom with two children—a third arrived a few years later—Robin was used to being able to get a really good coffee experience just down the street, yet found that element lacking in Vernon. To solve that problem, she opened Triumph Coffee in May 2014.

Triumph is located in a former dance studio along Vernon's main business strip on 30th Avenue. With 65 seats in the roomy 2,000-square-foot space, "you could easily have 10 strollers in here and they wouldn't be in the way," delights Hewitt. Triumph serves Bows & Arrows beans from Victoria, BC, in its espresso drinks. It alternates between Calgary's Phil & Sebastian Coffee Roasters and Vancouver's Elysian Coffee Roasters for its brewed options. Triumph also serves light lunches of soups, sandwiches, salads, quiches, cookies, muffins, and scones, all made from scratch daily by in-house bakers.

WILDCRAFT FOREST

1981 Highway 6, Lumby | 250-547-9812 | wildcraftforest.com

I've met my fair share of eccentric food people in my line of work. However, one thing I've learned over the past two decades of food writing is that today's fringe thinkers are often tomorrow's celebrated producers. (Collecting fireweed honey was once considered obsessive.) The other thing I've learned is that when these eccentrics seem to make sense *and* produce good food, I really need to pay attention.

This is what happened when I met DON ELZER, a wildcrafter. A what? I mistakenly asked him if this was the same as a forager, and he politely replied that he tries to encourage foragers to become wildcrafters so they can be better stewards of land and forests rather than just harvesters of wild products. A wildcrafter, I learned, *is* an expert in the harvesting and use of wild plants for food, medicine, design, and craft. A wildcrafter, however, is primarily concerned with protecting wild plants and wild medicines in their environment and harvesting lightly so as to keep the plants healthy and thriving. And then there's the educational process of passing on knowledge. In Elzer's words, "We link ancient wisdom and skills with science and storytelling."

I met Elzer on a rather cold, damp day in January when he kindly opened his studio on Highway 6 east of Lumby to me and my friend, writer Roslyne Buchanan, on one of our food road trips. We stamped our feet to stay warm as Elzer brewed Mulled Blood Moon wine for us. It contained botanicals collected from the nearby forest and fermented birch sap from his trees. He noted that he has botanical harvesting permission for a 15,000-acre area that extends from the North Okanagan into the Monashees. The hot drink was a curious mix of woody flavours, bitters, and botanicals. We also tasted Elzer's cold teas, which contained fascinating layers of pine, spruce, cedar, herbs, and fruit. I arrived skeptical and left with my own stash of wildcrafted dried tea mixes to try at home.

Don Elzer

DAVISON ORCHARDS COUNTRY VILLAGE

3111 Davison Road, Vernon | 250-549-3266 | davisonorchards.ca

I'll admit that I was a bit skeptical driving up to Davison Orchards given its "Country Village" Main Street exteriors. Then, at the 1944 farmhouse that is now the farm's café, I took my first bite of the handmade apple pie. A few seconds later, I stabbed my fork into the apple-berry-rhubarb pie my friend had ordered. Oh, this was some seriously good pie, with fruit from the farm and a handmade crust. I immediately planned my return trips for peach pie season (July through September) and pumpkin pie season (September and October). Pie, however, is just the start. There are also some really great farm-grown and handmade products on this multi-generation family farm.

In 1933, English immigrants Tom and May Davison paid a whopping $6,000 for a gently sloping piece of land facing south above the town of Vernon. They planted McIntosh and other popular apple varieties of the day: Wealthies, Dutches, and Delicious. A nephew, Bob Davison, began working on the farm in his late teens. In turn, he married and built a small cabin on the farm with his wife, Dora, and they took over the management of the farm. Bob and Dora raised their family of four children plus two foster children as the family grew apples for BC Fruit Shippers. In 1985, TOM DAVISON, Bob and Dora's son, and TAMRA DAVISON, Tom's wife, joined the farm, and the third-generation Davisons decided to direct-market their fruit, and whatever else they could grow, to the public. Thirty-plus years later, they do a roaring business from May 1 to October 31.

This fourth-generation family farm and orchard—Tom and Tamra's kids work in the family business now too—grows really good fresh fruit and ground crops. A visit here, especially the orchard tour, is a great way to learn about the Okanagan's fruit-growing history. Davison is known for its 25 different apple varieties, pumpkins, squash, peppers, tomatoes,

Tamra and Tom Davison

watermelon, cantaloupe, and other melons, all of which are for sale seasonally in the farm's market store along with various jams, jellies, and preserves made on-site from the farm's products. The UV-pasteurized apple juice is made from a blend of five different varieties, giving it a crisp, fresh apple taste. But seriously, try the pie. The Davisons sell over 2,000 handmade pies over the Thanksgiving weekend, for good reason.

HARTWOOD NORTH FARM

4462 Salmon River Road, Armstrong (by appointment only)

250-546-2701 | hartwoodnorthfarm.com

When asked what she likes best about the farming life, WENDY ARMSTRONG-TAYLOR replies, "Sitting beside Malcolm with a glass of wine, looking out at the farm at the end of our working day." Hartwood North Farm *is* a particularly beautiful farm, with its 110-year-old heritage house that she and husband MALCOLM TAYLOR have kept up since moving their family to the 67-acre farm in 2003. She's a landscape architect and it shows, not only in the farm's obvious aesthetic beauty but in the choice of products grown for markets in the North Okanagan region. The farm became certified organic in 2006 and Wendy dove into floriculture—she tends a thousand lavender plants, a mix of French and English lavender varieties—while Malcolm focuses on vegetable production. They also have a quarter of an acre of fruit trees and bush fruits as well as a 45-acre grain field on the property that is rotated through various grain crops throughout the years.

Not everyone considers the high cost of cut flowers. Large, commercial flower growers are said to be the heaviest users of agricultural chemicals, and pesticide residue is an often-overlooked concern. Since I'm a fan of cooking with flowers—I add them to fresh salads, infuse them in teas and lemonades, and garnish desserts with them—Hartwood North Farm is a bonanza of certified organic and spray-free flowers, with over 50 varieties. Of course, not all of them are culinary options. Wendy sells her flowers at the Vernon Farmers' Market on Thursdays and the Armstrong Farmers' Market on Saturdays, while Malcolm takes his organic veggies to Kelowna's Farmers' and Crafters' Market on Wednesdays and Saturdays. Root crops like beets, onions, and Japanese white (salad) turnips grow beautifully in the farm's light, sandy soils. While they're not set up for farm-gate sales, a visit to the farm can be arranged by phoning or emailing (via the website) ahead.

Wendy Armstrong-Taylor and Malcolm Taylor

YOU MIGHT ALSO LIKE

ARMSTRONG ASPARAGUS FARM and OKANAGAN ASPARAGUS FARM for just-picked, local asparagus daily throughout April, May, and early June. (Armstrong Asparagus: 4694 Knobhill Road, Armstrong, 250-546-9301, armstrongasparagus.com; Okanagan Asparagus: 4929 Lansdowne Road, Armstrong, 250-546-6634, okasparagus.com)

PILGRIMS' PRODUCE

1568 Eagle Rock Road, Armstrong | 250-546-3669 | pilgrimsproduce.com

ROBERT HETTLER grew up on a farm near Wetaskiwin, in central Alberta, and Robert's wife, KATHRYN, was raised "a city girl." After meeting in university, they spent six years in Northeast Brazil, where they participated in the agrarian land reform movements. Working conditions for rural farmers were poor there, and use of chemicals in large-scale agriculture was rampant. Kathryn remembers watching planes douse sugar cane fields with chemical insecticide, the same cane fields that would be harvested for commodity sugar. "The average life expectancy of villagers was 42 years," she says.

The Hettlers returned to Canada to farm their own land, determined to base their efforts on stewardship and direct sales to the community in which they would live. "We wanted to provide an alternative to conventional farming. We wanted to grow good food for our kids and our community," says Kathryn. They've been doing just this, through farmers' markets and their Community Supported Agriculture (CSA) program, since 1991 on their 14-acre farm in Armstrong.

After another trip to Brazil in 2005, the Hettlers returned with enthusiasm about permaculture ideas such as creating a "food forest" and further diversifying what foods they would grow, beyond annual vegetable crops and the usual fruit trees. They planted walnut, hazelnut, northern pecan, chestnut, and even Stone Pine nut trees. "Diversity is a good strategy to reduce risks," says Robert. Kathryn also adds that it's a wise response to the uncertainties around climate change. Now the food forest mindset is manifesting itself in other corners of the farm, with mulberries, elderberries, raspberries, Northline saskatoons, red currants, and even haskaps (see sidebar, page 43) scattered among the stone fruit trees.

Pilgrims' Produce is truly an asparagus-to-zucchini farm, with an impressive produce, fruit, and nut selection. The carrots, strawberries, and salad greens love the farm's sandy loam soil.

Kathryn and Rob Hettler, Carolyn and Mark Uher

Kathryn says there's been a "180-degree change" in the last few years in young people wanting to get into farming again. They have found a steady stream of young people wanting to work with them on their land, learn from Robert, and earn some money. Some of the young farmers currently working with them run the CSA program, in which customers buy a share in the farm's produce at the beginning of the year, giving them a steady stream of organic vegetables and fruit from spring to fall.

The haskap (also called a honeyberry) is an edible honeysuckle fruit that grows on shrubs and is native to northern Japan, Russia, and Canada. The flavour is unique but can be compared to a tart blueberry, a saskatoon berry, or even a raspberry. Haskaps have thin skin. Thanks to some varieties developed at the University of Saskatchewan, haskaps are being planted more widely as a commercial fruit crop in Canada.

Susan and Tony Van Den Tillaart

FIELDSTONE ORGANICS

4851 Schubert Road, Armstrong | 250-546-4558 | fieldstoneorganics.ca

TONY AND SUSAN VAN DEN TILLAART both grew up on farms. Raised on a mixed farm in BC that included dairy, meat, chickens, eggs, pork, and a garden, Tony eventually spent 30 years dairy farming in the North Okanagan, where he was careful with all inputs, like chemical fertilizers and livestock medications. "You know that they can't be good for you," he says. Susan grew up on a dairy farm in Ontario and had a background in healthcare. Together they knew that organic, health-focused agriculture was their path.

When the opportunity to start an organic grain farm and acquire some grain-hulling and seed-cleaning equipment came up, the Van Den Tillaarts formed a partnership with another like-minded local farmer, WILLEM ROELL, to start Fieldstone Organics in 2008. Access to their own cleaning and hulling machines gave Fieldstone total traceability and a fresher product with a smaller environmental footprint. "From day one, everything we do is for health. That's why we don't make or sell flour. When you break a kernel of grain, it starts to oxidize within two hours. A whole grain can last for years," explains Tony.

Fieldstone Organics currently works with about 25 other local organic farmers and now has a line of dozens of organic, non-GMO whole grain and whole seed products that are directly available to the consumer. (Fieldstone also sells wholesale to a number of organic BC brands of flour and cereal.) Situated in a lovely little shed, the on-site shop sells countertop mills and flakers as well as the full line of Fieldstone grains, like BC-grown organic barley, various wheats, oats, rye, and flax, as well as ancient grains like spelt, Einkorn wheat, Emmer wheat (also known as farro) and Khorasan wheat (also known under the brand-name Kamut®). Fieldstone also carries local organic lentils, dried peas, and other whole seed products like buckwheat.

FRESH VALLEY FARMS

1346 Mountain View Road, Armstrong (Fridays 12 PM to 7 PM or by appointment)

250-546-1101 | freshvalleyfarm.com

There is some rebellion against organic certification among certain farmers and meat producers who, in practice, are organic but don't go through the paper-trail hassle, not to mention the expense, of certification. (Through the course of this book, I learned that one of the main barriers to organic meat production is that certified organic feed is about three times as expensive as non-organic feed.) There's also the issue of what to do when an animal gets sick and legitimately needs antibiotics or other interventions.

I support certified organic farmers, but I'm just as comfortable buying meat from someone who encourages me to pop up to his or her farm whenever I want, like STEVE MEGGAIT at Fresh Valley Farms, even though the meats are not certified organic.

Meggait really cares that people are connected with where their food comes from, and he knows it's challenging to find a meat producer with an open-door policy. The fact that you can visit and see with your own eyes that Meggait farms sustainably, ethically, and organically is much more reassuring to me than a stamp on a package. He also has misgivings about what he calls the "factorization of organics" and the carbon footprint that some types of organic certification demand (with feed that comes mostly from the EU, for instance). To reduce the carbon footprint of the meat he produces, he feeds his animals with local grains sourced from friends and neighbours who grow without herbicides and pesticides. He grazes his animals on his farm's pastureland—"it's what cows were meant to eat," he says—and has an open-door policy that allows customers to visit the farm to see how the broiler chickens, Angus cows, and Berkshire-Tamworth pigs are being raised.

Meggait is a fourth-generation Okanagan farmer. His father and grandfather still breed cattle on an adjacent farm, and Meggait finishes

Steve Meggait

the cattle on pasture at his farm. Fresh Valley Farms' meat is available direct from the farm and through a Community Supported Agriculture meat program called the Homesteader Box, or at farmers' markets in Vernon, Coldstream, and Armstrong.

HELMUT'S SAUSAGE KITCHEN

2103 48 Avenue, Vernon | 250-260-3281 | helmutssausagekitchen.ca

My chef friends talk about this place so much, I joke that it should be renamed Hel-*must*'s. It has an old-school vibe, likely because the owner, HELMUT WEST, grew up learning the business from his German-born father, who learned sausage making and meat smoking from his father. West grew up in Vernon, but left for Germany after high school, where he formalized his training as a butcher and sausage maker. The beauty and pace of life in Vernon drew him back, and he opened Helmut's Sausage Kitchen, a processor of specialty smoked meats and sausages, in 2001.

This place speaks to the large flow of post-war immigration to Vernon from Germany and Eastern Europe and Holland—the Ukrainian Ham Sausage, a best-seller, uses a recipe that dates back 300 years—but also reflects a more global outlook with selections like the spicy Mexican chorizo or Tunisian lamb sausage. The Okanagan apricot and pork sausages and the sparkling apple and cider sausages speak to the local landscape.

The original Vernon location is still where local pork and beef are cured and smoked into several dozen types of European sausages, salamis, and cured products. Beyond the meats, there's a large selection of Old World condiments like pickles, mustards, and relishes, as well as a good selection of German candies. The Kelowna location (1875 Commerce Avenue, on Highway 97; 250-861-3281) has a hot deli with cafeteria-style dining.

48

Helmut's Sausage Kitchen, Vernon location

WHEN YOU'RE HUNGRY IN THE NORTH OKANAGAN,
YOU MIGHT LIKE TO TRY:

DJ'S PEROGIE KITCHEN, for some seriously great handmade perogies. (4409 29th Street, Vernon, 250-542-6165)

FRIESEN'S COUNTRYTYME GARDENS, for the epic breakfasts and the out-of-the-way home cooking and produce market that is the stuff of Sunday outings. (9172 Kalamalka Road, Coldstream, 250-549-3587)

THE NAKED PIG BARBECUE AND SMOKEHOUSE, for a local spin on barbecue and grill. (2933 30th Avenue, Vernon, 778-475-5475, nakedpig.ca)

STATION BBQ SMOKEHOUSE, for BBQ aficionados. I was tipped off by Andrew McWilliam of Ratio Coffee & Pastry, who advised that the owners of this eatery are "as excited about barbecue as I am about coffee." (101-3131 29th Street, Vernon, 250-260-6677, stationbbq.com)

THE WILD OAK CAFÉ AND COMMUNITY MARKET, for housemade soups, sandwiches, espresso drinks, salads, and goodies. You can also pick up frozen beef, lamb, chicken, and pork. (2539 Pleasant Valley Road, Armstrong, 778-442-2028)

ROSEBANK FARMS

4218 Wyatt Road, Armstrong | 250-546-2712; 250-546-2733 | rosebankfarms.ca

ANDREA AND STEPHEN GUNNER moved to Armstrong 25 years ago because, as Andrea puts it, "the pace of life here is human scale." She came from the West Coast and he from the Fraser Valley. Wanting to farm and raise a family (now three young adults), they established Rosebank Farms, a nine-acre property. They experimented with some crops and livestock, but eventually settled on pasture-raising chickens and turkeys. Andrea says that Rosebank Farms now feeds about 500 households in the Thompson Okanagan region.

Unlike most poultry operations I've been to, the Gunners happily welcome their customers to their farm. "It keeps us sharp," Andrea says. It's also a way for the Gunners to explain the "agro-forestry" model they use for raising poultry. It's a free-range scenario where chickens and turkeys dine as much as they wish on the variety of vegetation and insects in the mixed woodland-grassland areas. This is how Rosebank Farms' poultry gets about 15 to 20 percent of their diet—from pecking around at grasses, other vegetation, worms, and insects. The rest comes from the grains and oilseeds the Gunners select as feed. The birds are leaner and have less fat, and the eggs have a lovely yellow yolk from their vitamin A- and omega-3-rich pasture diet. In return, the Gunners have watched as the thin glacial till of their land fattens into lush pasture whenever the flock moves on, scratches and pecks at the soil, then leaves behind nitrogen-rich natural fertilizer. While Rosebank Farms is open to visitors and customers, Andrea also delivers in the region, often meeting up with customers in parking lots.

Andrea also runs an agricultural consulting business—she's an agricultural economist—from her on-farm office, and she's very optimistic about good food in the North Okanagan. She's especially encouraged by the recent influx of 20- to 30-year-olds in the area, many of whom have come to farm, and others who are arriving for a quality of life that

Stephen Gunner

is hard to access elsewhere. "If you scratch a bit at its sleepy little farm town exterior," she notes, "there's an interesting counterculture and an emerging arts culture here."

THE WILD MOON
ORGANICS COMPANY

1199 Mountain View Road, Armstrong (no farm-gate sales) | 778-212-6497 | wildmoon.org

I first heard about RICHARD QUIRING at the Wild Moon Organics Company from chef Mark Filatow. I'm a huge fan of the charcuterie Filatow makes at his restaurant, Waterfront Wines, in Kelowna, and I know he has high standards for his suppliers. It is easy to see why Wild Moon Organics' heritage Berkshire pork and Belted Galloway beef are making their way onto the menus of the valley's best restaurants. Luckily, there's enough Wild Moon Organics Company meat available for the rest of us.

A few decades ago in Saskatchewan, Quiring took over the family business—commercial hog farming. "It was all about numbers," he says of the 10,000-hog operation, noting that theirs was considered a relatively small hog farm on the commercial scale of things. "You know what?" he adds, "We didn't eat pork." Having no interest in the white, dry, tasteless meat that resulted from commercially raised pigs, he eventually got out of pig farming completely.

"Four years ago, we were determined that we were going to live in the Okanagan. We were going to raise our food organically, and we were going to live more sustainably," Quiring says of his family's 2011 decision to buy 190 acres of land that ranges from fertile fields to mountain pastures, forest, and creeks, all near the town of Armstrong. Quiring's son, TRISTAN QUIRING, was a keen researcher and made the case for Berkshire pigs, a hardy black-haired and black-skinned heritage breed that is seeing a resurgence on small-scale farms. Berkshires have a gentle disposition, are keen foragers, and thrive in natural outdoor expanses. Their meat is sought after because of its good fat content and darker, richer flavour. The Quirings also raise a small herd of Belted Galloway, a Scottish heritage cattle breed known for its flavourful, well-marbled meat.

Tristan and Richard Quiring

In 2015, the Quirings built an on-farm commercial kitchen and pro-cessing facility to make full use of the animal by-products after slaughter. This includes making a high-quality, certified organic bone broth and rendering certified organic lard. "Lard is being re-appreciated," says Richard enthusiastically. Once the broth is made, the bones will be used for an organic dog food product. "It'll be a zero-waste facility!"

The transition from a conventional commodity farm with 10,000 hogs to a certified organic farm with a 500-pig capacity on 190 acres has been all about sustainability. "For me, it's a whole new chapter in life. I'm determined to demonstrate that small-scale, organic farming is sustainable when done right," says Richard. Wild Moon Organics Company isn't set up for farm-gate sales, but you can order online on their website (Kelowna pick-up) or find Richard at farmers' markets in Kelowna and Vernon.

Melissa and David Dobernigg, and family

THE BX PRESS

4667 East Vernon Road, Vernon | 250-503-2163 | thebxpress.com

DAVID AND MELISSA DOBERNIGG are the third generation on David's family's orchard in Vernon. The Doberniggs have three girls of their own—the fourth generation running through the lines of trees.

Most of the 30 acres of apples on the Doberniggs' farm go to BC Tree Fruits' packing plants or to fresh pasteurized juice that is pressed and packed on-farm. About 10 percent of the apple crop, however, is dedicated to the cidery—though based on the first two years' success, they might have to bump up that percentage. The BX Press Cidery & Orchard opened its beautiful tasting room in May 2014 and was completely sold out of its 12,000-bottle inventory by August. It's no wonder. With none of the syrupy sweet style that early Okanagan ciders adopted, BX Press ciders are crisp, dry, and clean-tasting. True cider apples go into the Prospector, a tart English-style brew. The CrackWhip is dry-hopped just before bottling, which gives it a pleasing bite. And a dash of natural cherry juice gives the Bandit its rose-coloured blush and dark fruit depth, without the sweetness.

HONEYMOON MEADERY

5011 Bella Vista Road, Vernon | 250-542-8088 | planetbee.com

My beverage palate runs screaming from sweetness and toward anything dry, tannic, or even bitter. And mead is what I would consider an acquired taste. In other words, I'm still waiting for my mead conversion. That said, Honeymoon Meadery's general manager and meadmaker, MARTIN HENDERSON, assured me that there is something for everyone—even me—in his extensive mead line. To my surprise, he was right. I was taken with the Parad Ice Berry Mead, with its clean raspberry and boysenberry flavours and without the cloying sweetness of an icewine. (It makes a great pairing with a cheese plate!)

Honeymoon Meadery is an offshoot of Planet Bee Honey Farm in Vernon (see page 20). The tasting room shares a space with Planet Bee's busy retail shop. Honeymoon Meadery uses 100 percent BC honey, 90 percent of which is Planet Bee's own local wildflower honey, gathered by beekeeper and Planet Bee owner ED NOWEK's hives at various locations around Vernon.

Honeymoon Meadery at Planet Bee Honey Farm

YOU MIGHT ALSO LIKE

MARTEN BREWING COMPANY, sister business of Naked Pig (see page 49).
Though not yet open at the time of press, it looks like a promising addition to
the craft brewing scene in the north given that Stefan Buhl, former brewmaster
at Kelowna's Tree Brewing, has been hired here. (2933 30th Avenue, Vernon,
250-718-0996, martenbrewpub.com)

OKANAGAN SPIRITS

5204 24th Street, Vernon | 250-549-3120 | okanaganspirits.com

As mentioned in the introduction, every locavore foodie in BC who enjoys a mid-afternoon G&T, a pre-dinner martini, a pear eau-de-vie, or a post-feasting grappa owes a debt of gratitude to Okanagan Spirits. It's been instrumental—no, monumental—in the current craft distillery movement we're all now enjoying.

Okanagan Spirits began in the early 2000s when Frank Deiter, a German distiller who was nearing retirement age in Vernon, couldn't believe that so much local fruit was left unused. He applied for a distillery licence in 2004 and Okanagan Spirits was born as a pioneering small-batch microdistillery that used a wood-fired copper pot still (nothing dangerous about that!) and all Okanagan fruits. The regulations were crazy-making, as were the economics of producing small-batch craft spirits. But Okanagan Spirits persevered, and Deiter garnered international awards for its excellent products. I first fell in love with the fruit liqueurs like the blackcurrant, the cranberry, and the red raspberry. From there I progressed to the gin, the vodka, the absinthe, and the rest of its line of 25 spirits. Okanagan Spirits now makes a single malt whisky so popular that it's available for purchase only through an annual lottery.

With a change in ownership as of 2010, Okanagan Spirits just keeps rising. In 2013, at the World Spirits Award in Klagenfurt, Austria, it won Spirit of the Year and Distillery of the Year and achieved a World Class Distillery designation. Okanagan Spirits owner TONY DYCK, chief executive officer TYLER DYCK, and senior distiller PETER VON HAHN were ecstatic about the confirmation that a family-owned distillery in the North Okanagan could not only hold its own in an international competition, but come out on top in key categories. When the question arose in 2015 of whether to enter the competition again, Tony admits they carefully considered the risk of not being able to match the 2013

COURTESY OF OKANAGAN SPIRITS

Clockwise from top left: Peter Von Hahn, Tony Dyck, and Tyler Dyck

result. "But Peter came to us, and he's usually very modest. He felt very strongly about what he'd done over the past year."

They decided that von Hahn would travel to the World Spirits Awards in March 2015 in Køge, Denmark. Eight of Okanagan Spirits' top products would be up against 300-some entries from 64 other distilleries in 25 countries. Von Hahn was right—every one of Okanagan Spirits' entries received a medal. Laird of Fintry became Canada's first single malt whisky to win gold at this event. Both the Haskap Liqueur and the

Danish-style Aquavitus won "double-gold" medals, and the Blackcurrant Liqueur triumphed as Spirit of the Year in the fruit brandy category. Moreover, the distiller renewed its World Class Distillery designation and took home Distillery of the Year again in the fruit brandy category.

Meanwhile, back in Vernon, it was all hands on deck for the move of Okanagan Spirits to its brand new 16,000-square-foot custom-built distillery with tasting bars, a whisky lounge, and even a theatre for educational tours. The medals and trophies on the shelves look good, as does the impressive 50-column still that is so tall it requires its own skylight. The new distillery opened in April 2015. Okanagan Spirits also has a tasting room in downtown Kelowna (267 Bernard Avenue, 778-484-5174).

CRAFT DISTILLERS GUILD OF BC

Okanagan Spirits CEO Tyler Dyck heads up the Craft Distillers Guild of BC (craftdistillersbc.ca), now 23 members strong. This group was instrumental in lobbying the province to change the antiquated liquor laws that were stifling the industry. The new regulatory framework is responsible for the boom of distilleries in the province. As most distillers will tell you, it's just the beginning. I'm sure that as this book goes to print, I'll be adding new entries of excellent craft distilleries, and undoubtedly more will open just as the ink is drying on these pages.

→ **FARTHER AFIELD** ←

CRANNÓG ALES

706 Elson Road, Sorrento (tours and tastings Friday and Saturday afternoons
by appointment only) | 250-675-6847 | crannogales.com

There are two beermakers in Sorrento in the Shuswap region, which
spreads north from the Okanagan, who have my undying adoration and
gratitude. BRIAN MACISAAC AND REBECCA KNEEN started Crannóg Ales
in 2000 on their 10-acre certified organic farm, making it Canada's first
certified organic farmhouse microbrewery.

From the get-go, it's been all about sustainability, and they've held
their line beautifully, resisting growth beyond what they need to pay the
bills, compensate suppliers, and keep a bit of change in their pockets as
profit for their labours. They have a diversified farm called Left Fields
Farm (not to be confused with Left Field Cider Company in Logan Lake,
see below), where they produce fruit and vegetables, raise livestock, and
grow their own line of hops for the brewery. Their livestock (pigs, sheep,
chickens) dine on spent mash from the brewing process. The water for
the beer comes out of a well at the centre of their property, and they
only supply kegs (no bottles) to locations within driving distance.

Luckily, the Okanagan *is* within driving distance, and you can have
a pint pulled at various pubs and restaurants in Vernon, Kelowna,
and Summerland, and as far south as the Kettle Valley Station Pub in
Penticton. If I had to pick just one, and thankfully I do not, I'd choose
the rich coffee-and-chocolatey Back Hand of God Stout as the keg to
be marooned with on a desert island.

LEFT FIELD CIDER COMPANY

Highway 97C between Logan Lake and Merritt | 250-448-6991 | leftfieldcider.com

Again, while technically outside the Okanagan, I wanted to include the excellent cidermaking team at Left Field Cider Company. It's worth the detour to
taste the British-influenced, crisp, clean ciders here made from English and
French cider apples blended with Okanagan and Shuswap dessert varieties.

JEREMY LUYPEN

Predator Ridge Resort | 301 Village Centre Place, Vernon

1-855-541-7929 | predatorridge.com

JEREMY LUYPEN came to Kelowna in 1995 on a basketball scholarship as he pursued his Bachelor of Arts at the University of British Columbia Okanagan. He's since put his stamp on many restaurants in the valley, from the Hotel Eldorado to Passa Tempo at Spirit Ridge Resort in Osoyoos. When he opened Terrafina at Hester Creek Winery in Oliver as owner-chef in 2011, it was named one of the Top 20 Winery Restaurants in the World by *Wine Access* magazine.

Luypen is now in charge of five kitchen outlets at Predator Ridge Resort, a 1,000-home golf course community a 15-minute drive south of Vernon along Highway 97. Perhaps the best representation of his food philosophy is Range Lounge & Grill, where Okanagan-raised hormone-free beef and sustainable seafood anchor the menu. The leafy greens and vegetables are from his favourite local farms. "We buy at least nine whole cows a year," Luypen explains, as it helps sustain local farms if they can sell more than just striploins from their animals. He does the same with pigs, and he supports many local quality producers like Farmcrest Foods in Salmon Arm, Sterling Springs Chickens in Falkland, North Okanagan Game Meats in Enderby, Codfathers Seafood Market in Kelowna, and Lake Country Culinary Farms for edible flowers, fresh herbs, lettuce, tomatoes, and kale. "We're a restaurant that happens to be at a golf course," he says, but his menus certainly defy any expectations of "clubhouse dining." As an instructor at Okanagan College, Luypen also teaches and mentors cooks and apprentices.

Generous with their time, Luypen and his wife, Jessica Spelliscy, support various charity causes such as their own J Project (jproject-kelowna.com), which they began in partnership with the Society of Hope, the largest non-profit provider of social housing in the BC Interior. The J Project cooks meals for seniors who are unable to get out to shop or

Jeremy Luypen

cook for themselves and solicits donations for gifts for these seniors. Many Kelowna-area chef colleagues quietly help the J Project in these endeavours, especially around Christmastime.

FARMERS' MARKETS

This information was correct at the time of press, but I've provided web addresses whenever possible so you can check the hours and locations before you visit.

ARMSTRONG FARMERS' MARKET

3371 Pleasant Valley Road (IPE Fairgrounds)

Saturdays, late April to end of October, 8 AM to 12 PM

markets.bcfarmersmarket.org/market/armstrong-farmers-market

AVENUE MARKET, VERNON

30th Avenue, 3000 block to 3300 block

Fridays, May to September, 4 PM to 8 PM

downtownvernon.com/events/avenue-market/

CHERRYVILLE FARMERS' MARKET

Highway 6, Cherryville, on the grounds of the

Cherryville Artisans Shop Gallery & Marketplace

Saturdays, April to October, 9 AM to 1 PM

farmersmarket@cherryville.net

COLDSTREAM FARMERS' MARKET

9909 Kal Lake Road

Wednesdays, April to October, 2:30 PM to 6 PM

facebook.com/coldstreamfarmersmarket

VERNON FARMERS' MARKET

3445 43rd Avenue

Mondays and Thursdays, mid-April to late October, 8 AM to 1 PM

vernonfarmersmarket.ca

CENTRAL OKANAGAN

LAKE COUNTRY

KELOWNA

OYAMA

PEACHLAND

WEST KELOWNA

CENTRAL OKANAGAN

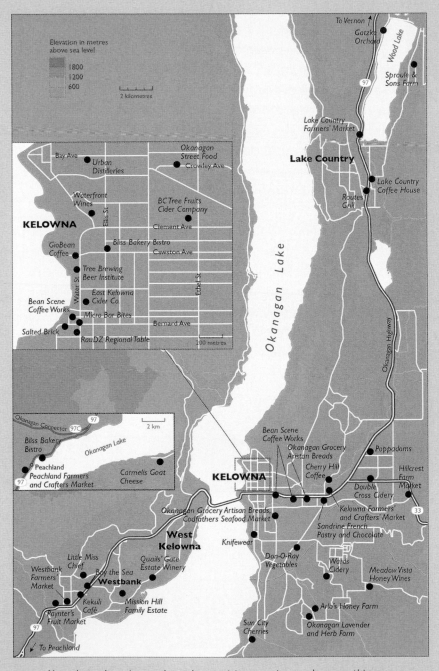

Note that only artisans who welcome visitors on site are shown on this map.

L AKE COUNTRY IS ABOUT AS idyllic as it gets. Family farms and orchards give it the title "Apple Capital of Canada," and you're never far from a sandy beach and the blue, blue water of Wood, Kalamalka, and Okanagan Lakes. U-picks, fruit stands, and independent coffee houses are where tourists and locals alike gather.

Kelowna is considered "the big city" in the Okanagan, but it's a big city built around a thriving culinary culture—from wineries and vineyards to orchards, farms, and sophisticated fine dining. It's the culinary epicentre of the region, cosmopolitan and multicultural without being overwhelming.

South of the bridge in West Kelowna are 1950s-era fruit stands and the historic Gellatly Nut Farm, a stone fruit's throw from the iconic bell tower of Mission Hill Family Estate Winery, which announced to the world that Okanagan wines were ambitious and world class.

Peachland, at the bend of the lake across from Rattlesnake Island and Okanagan Mountain Provincial Park, is a step back again in time, with its laid-back waterfront drive, beaches, cafés, and lakefront restaurants.

LAKE COUNTRY HARVEST

6948 McCoubrey Road, Lake Country (no on-site sales)

250-470-7759 | lakecountryharvest.com

PAULA DIAKIW goes by the moniker "the Cherry Godmother." Her summer-season workers, mostly teens and young adults, are "the Fruit Ninjas" and have T-shirts that declare "Our job is the pits." Together they clean, pit, dry, and preserve fruit from a handful of Lake Country Farms so that we can stir some dried peach chips into our winter oatmeal in the depths of January.

When Diakiw—a self-declared "jammer" since she was 12—moved to the Okanagan from Jasper, Alberta, in 2006 (and before that she lived in Vancouver for 30 years), she was astonished at how much high-quality fresh fruit in the valley went to waste. "We have enough fruit to feed all of Canada, but not all of Canada can get to it right away," she says. "There are so many ways to extend the life of fruit." The other surplus she noticed in her rural, agricultural neighbourhood was teenagers hanging around in their basements playing video games during the summer. Lake Country Harvest was born in 2010.

Diakiw got to know her neighbours, many of whom had been in the orchard business for decades, and offered to pay them for their fruit, which was especially helpful during short, plentiful seasons when the local market is flooded with so many fresh fruits that last only a few days once picked. She then gutted and converted a double garage on her property into a gleaming, spacious commercial kitchen. She hired local teens to pit, peel, and dry strawberries, blueberries, cherries, apricots, peaches, apples, pears, and plums. She kept them motivated and fed with regular smoothie breaks and as taste testers for her product line.

Diakiw cherishes the relationships she's developed with her skilful and sustainability-minded fruit-growing neighbours. She labels her peach preserves as "Alma's Peaches" after Alma Fochler, the orchardist Diakiw

Serena Fochler of Fochler's orchard and Paula Diakiw

buys peaches from and whose family has been growing fruit on the same land for over 70 years. The cherries come from Sal and Claudette Tangaro of Tangaro Orchards, 10 minutes down the road. One summer, Diakiw and her Fruit Ninjas pitted 3,600 kilograms (8,000 pounds) of cherries alone. The teens who work for her have come back summer after summer.

Lake Country Harvest's product line now includes muesli, jams, jellies, fruit vinegars, and artisan cordial syrups like Peach-Earl Grey and Blueberry-Lime.

Helen Kennedy

ARLO'S HONEY FARM

4329 Bedford Lane, Kelowna | 250-764-2883 | arloshoneyfarm.com

Wear something dark, especially brown or black, and you look like a bear to even the docile honeybee. Never stand at the mouth of a hive, blocking the bees' flight path. Bees get cranky with wind. Not that you need to worry about any of this at Arlo's Honey Farm. A handy viewing gallery with a Plexiglas window separates beekeeper and market gardener HELEN KENNEDY from any group who schedules an on-farm tour. She explains the needs and behaviour of her bees and how they forage on Dutch white clover, various market garden vegetables, and the flower blossoms that the Kennedys now plant on their farm as a food source for their bees, from the early spring crocuses all the way to the pre-winter blossoms.

Kennedy grew up on a farm in Alberta and came back to her agricultural roots after a career in finance and management. In 2000, she bought a 14-acre hay farm in Kelowna, and after a couple of false starts—an expensive one with grapes—she settled on planting her land with a 5-acre market garden and on keeping bees. She had no prior experience with bees, so the first three years "were a bit rocky." Now Arlo's Honey Farm has a steady stream of agritourists who come for Kennedy's bee talks, Arlo's buttery yellow and thick honey, and the farm-gate sales of everything from asparagus in the early spring to haskap berries, raspberries, gooseberries, beets, shell peas, edible pea pods, carrots, onions, and 45 varieties of garlic. The bees, however, "are the nucleus of the farm," says Kennedy. Everything else she does revolves around them.

BLISS BAKERY BISTRO

4200 Beach Avenue, Peachland | 250-767-2711 | blissbakery.ca

Just a quick turn off the highway and two blocks in and you're on the corner of 13th Street and Beach Avenue in Peachland. For over a decade now, BARRY AND DARCI YEO's Bliss Bakery Bistro has been making artisan breads by hand, daily, and serving good fair-trade, organic espresso coffees with Kelowna's Cherry Hill Coffee.

I love that Bliss is all about the details since its opening day in 2005. The Yeos proudly announce that they wash their lettuce—no prewashed spring mix with stabilizing gas preservative here. They roast their own chicken, beef, and pork with their own spice rub for their sandwiches. They make their daily soups from scratch—no pre-scrubbed or-peeled vegetables—and they make their own stock from their organic roasted chickens. Remember to look up from your plate at least once to take in the lakeshore view.

Bliss Bakery Bistro's Kelowna location is 1289 Ellis Street (Ellis and Cawston); 778-484-5355. Their main catering location and bakery is tucked away in an industrial zone in West Kelowna but has a grab-and-go counter, Mondays to Fridays, at 1405 Stevens Road, West Kelowna; 778-755-5801.

Darci and Barry Yeo

OKANAGAN GROCERY ARTISAN BREADS

2355 Gordon Drive (main shop), 1979 Windsor Road (bake shop), Kelowna

250-862-2811 (main shop), 250-868-4929 (bake shop) | okanagangrocery.com

I find it hard to believe that MONIKA WALKER, owner and bread maven at Okanagan Grocery, failed her first bread-baking exam at culinary school. She grew up in Germany in a household where afternoon cake and coffee were a daily ritual. She remembers baking cheesecake and other coffee cakes as young as six, thinking that was normal. While at Dubrulle International Culinary & Hotel Institute (now the Art Institute of Vancouver), she studied professional cooking, and she went into fine dining restaurants as a keen young chef. The trouble was, she was miserable. She headed to Vancouver to work at Mix the Bakery and was immediately hooked on breadmaking. Walker's husband, Bill, negotiated a job for her at Okanagan Grocery Artisan Breads, which was started by Rhys Pender and Alishan Driediger in Kelowna in 2003. Soon Walker was working full time, and then she bought Okanagan Grocery in 2007 when Pender and Driediger sold to open Little Farm, their own winery in Cawston. By 2011, it was time for Walker to expand with a second location and the bakery's new kitchen on Spall Road in the Ambrosi neighbourhood.

Okanagan Grocery has remained the top bread stop in Kelowna (and well worth the drive from other parts of the valley) for its incredible traditional *levain* breads. The sourdough starters even have their own names: Arnold, who Walker says is "ancient," and Naomi, who is about 12 years old now. (Don't worry, it's a breadmaker thing to name your starters. They are alive and require regular attention, so you might as well give them names to go with their demanding personalities.) Aside from pieces of Arnold or Naomi, the loaves are made with raw, unbleached, organic, local white flour bought from Rogers Foods, a 60-plus-year-old mill in Armstrong. Then, depending on the recipe, Walker or her four

Monika Walker

other bakers add rye flour, seeds, or other natural ingredients. Each loaf is made and shaped by hand. Loaves are cooked off in the stone deck oven that you can see as you walk into the larger bake shop location.

A regular daily roster of breads features baguette, rosemary focaccia, the Okanagan Grocery Loaf, and even the Callebaut Chocolate Loaf. Wednesday is Bavarian Pretzel day. Thursday is Peanut Butter & Jelly Loaf. Friday is Organic Apple Raisin Sourdough and Asiago & Black Pepper Loaf. Saturday is all-butter croissants, pain au chocolate, and brioche. Okanagan Grocery also carries a great selection of artisan cheeses from the valley, preserves, and other products, making it a bit of an artisan food hub in Kelowna.

The only time I have ever made a loaf that even comes close to one of Walker's is when I took her breadmaking class at the bakeshop. And I'm not entirely sure that she didn't switch out my misshapen attempt for a more respectable *boule* at the end of the class.

Ofri Barmor

CARMELIS GOAT CHEESE

170 Timberline Road, Kelowna | 250-764-9033 | carmelisgoatcheese.com

OFRI AND OFER BARMOR moved with their two daughters from Israel to Canada in 2003. They bought a little cottage farm property in the wooded hills near CedarCreek Estate Winery and St. Hubertus Estate Winery in Kelowna's southeast corner adjacent to Okanagan Mountain Park. They wanted to raise goats and make French-style goat cheeses as they had in Israel, so they went about building the necessary facilities and acquiring a herd. Four days after the goats arrived, the devastating Okanagan Mountain Park forest fire in August 2003 reduced their cellar, barn, and cheese boutique to ashes. Thankfully, the goats and their family home were saved, but the fire consumed everything else.

Remarkably, their vision for Carmelis survived. The Barmors rebuilt and are now over a decade into producing 20-some exquisite artisan goat cheeses with the 100-goat herd that roams their property and loves to greet you on your way to the cheese shop. Ofri makes all her cheeses by hand, and they're aged in the extensive cheese cave, controlled for temperature and humidity. As a gelato fan, I am also always intrigued to choose from their gelato flavours—yes, made from goat milk. Note: Carmelis is closed November through February.

PETER JOHNER
SWISS CHOCOLATIER

Lake Country (orders by phone or email only) | 250-766-1918

pjohner.chocolatier@gmail.com

PETER JOHNER learned the chocolatier trade in his native Switzerland as a 15-year-old apprentice. He went on with his training there, both in cooking and as a professional restaurateur, before bringing his culinary standards to Edmonton. I've known him since, well, forever it seems. Now he has joined the ranks of so many Albertans by retiring to Lake Country, just a few miles from Gray Monk Estate Winery (also owned and run by transplanted European Albertans in the Okanagan). But Johner hasn't completely retired. He's in business seasonally between Christmas and Easter with his handmade Swiss truffles with creamy wine-filled centres and his crunchy nut and nougat pralines. My personal favourite is his orange hazelnut dark chocolate bark.

Peter Johner

Sandrine Martin-Raffault

SANDRINE FRENCH PASTRY & CHOCOLATE

1865 Dilworth Drive, Kelowna | 250-860-1202 | sandrinepastry.com

SANDRINE MARTIN-RAFFAULT's family in Lyon, France, has been in pastry and chocolate for generations. When she left her career in finance to find a better balance, her husband, Pierre-Jean, spearheaded the idea to move to Canada.

They started out with a business in Kelowna called La Boulangerie Gourmet Café in 2004, hiring breadmakers from France and with Sandrine running the sweet kitchen and Pierre-Jean the savoury. But the scope was too wide, the hours were insane, and Sandrine's heart was in the pastry side of the business, not the bread. They sold La Boulangerie and opened Sandrine in May 2010, focusing on classic and traditional French pastry and chocolate as you would find in a pâtisserie in France. (She started making macarons nine years ago and waited patiently until the craze finally hit North America. Now she has a suspicion that we're going to see croquembouches and religieuses—éclairs with coloured icing—replace the macaron as the new must-have French pastries.) Sandrine adheres to traditional French methods, pure ingredients, and time-consuming techniques; otherwise, she wouldn't feel confident in her products. She declares that her taste memories from France and her family's pâtisserie DNA just won't let her do things any differently. She is an artisan in her genes and says that you can "taste it right away" when someone doesn't love making pastry.

First there are the chocolates, about two dozen kinds. I'm partial to the salted caramel dark chocolate and the passion fruit dark chocolate. Then there are handmade croissants, palmiers, mille-feuilles Napoleon, pain au chocolate, gateaux, cookies, macarons, and other pastry confections. While she mostly resists any trends from this side of the pond, you can find a few jams and jellies made with local fruits, and even one plum-beer jam made with Tree Brewing beer.

BEAN SCENE COFFEE WORKS

Bean Scene HQ–Roastery, Bakery, and Retail | 1615 Dickson Avenue, Kelowna | 778-484-5445

Bean Scene Downtown–Mother Ship | 274 Bernard Avenue, Kelowna | 250-763-1814

Bean Scene Central | 1835 Gordon Drive, Kelowna | 250-860-7818 | beanscene.ca

DEB SYNNOT AND JOHN ANDERSON have been called Kelowna's coffee power couple, which strikes me as funny, as they both have a very relaxed, hippie-style vibe, which is all the more impressive given their love of espresso.

Anderson is the original roaster at Bean Scene, and he established the flavour profiles of the single-origin coffees that go into Bean Scene coffee. This former waterworks construction professional also has an obvious engineering bent; he invented his own wet scrubber exhaust system for the Probat in order to eliminate over 1.2 million BTUs in natural gas per hour during roasting. Not only is this an impressive energy reduction, it also reduces the fire risk and doesn't flood the neighbourhood with the smell of roasting coffee, which is nice from time to time, but I imagine could be a bit much every day, all day. For his invention, he won a City of Kelowna environmental award for business innovation. The Probat roaster is in full view of the open, high-ceiling headquarters where the baking and roasting take place. Green beans slowly turn to glossy brown in 12-kilogram (26-pound) batches.

In 2012, AMY AND AL LANG were looking to get into the coffee business. Amy had been running the Bean Scene bakery for a number of years and Al had experience in food and hospitality. They struck a deal with Synnot and Anderson to buy and run Bean Scene Central. A year later, they bought Bean Scene HQ. In 2015, the Langs became full partners in the business with Synnot and Anderson and Al has been taking over roasting duties from Anderson.

Besides the roaster, Bean Scene is also a bakery and deli. They source locally whenever possible, and only real, recognizable ingredients go into

Al Lang and Deb Synnot

their scones, cookies, salads, sandwiches, and "bowls." My personal fave is the Thai-inspired, high-protein, high-taste Buddha's bowl for when I'm racing around in Kelowna between appointments and need a healthy, quick lunch.

YOU MIGHT ALSO LIKE

CHERRY HILL COFFEE, for the premium beans they've been hand-roasting for over a quarter century. The certified organic Arabica beans speak to a commitment to quality and sustainability. There's an on-site espresso bar and retail shop, and facility tours are available. (1404 Hunter Court, Kelowna, 250-861-4733, cherryhillcoffee.com)

GIOBEAN COFFEE, where the baristas pull perfect espresso drinks every time. This is definitely a local fave for coffee aficionados. (1320 Water Street, Kelowna, 250-868-2992, giobeancoffee.com)

LAKE COUNTRY COFFEE HOUSE

10356 Bottom Wood Lake Road, Lake Country | 250-766-9006 | lakecountrycoffee.com

People come from miles around just for the ultimate square of classic carrot cake with cream cheese icing. At least this is how I first heard about SEAN AND CAROL SPROULE's Lake Country Coffee House. Carol won't discuss the recipe—I respect that—except to say that the carrots are organic and that less is more. If I had a recipe like that, I'd keep it close to my chest as well.

Lake Country Coffee House is a second career for both Sean and Carol. Sean, a local Okanaganite, was driving truck, and Carol, a Maritimer, was working in healthcare and living on Vancouver Island. Each had lost their spouse, but family members on both sides engaged in some old-fashioned matchmaking, rekindling a romance "from when we were both kids," as Carol tells it. Soon they were married and looking for a career that would let them work together. Sean's cousins had opened Lake Country Coffee House in 2010 and were looking to sell it that same year, so Carol and Sean bought the business and dove headlong into their new role as owners and operators of a 50-seat coffee house. It shares its space with the Lake Country Public Art Gallery and is housed in a former butcher shop located across from the Aspen Grove Golf Course on Bottom Wood Lake Road. The meat racks—now painted glossy black—are a real conversation starter, laughs Carol.

Lake Country Coffee House serves organic Cherry Hill Coffee, roasted in Kelowna. The Sproules buy most of their preserves, sauces, and breads that aren't made in-house from vendors at local farmers' markets. The yogurt in their parfaits and the cheese served with various dishes are from Jerseyland Organics in nearby Grand Forks, and the bread and spelt pizza crust are made by Urs Baumann, a local baker. Brigitte Gysi makes the beloved sunflower flax sandwich bread. "We know who makes our food," says Carol, adding that independent coffee houses and cafés like theirs can run with high food costs only

Carol and Sean Sproule

if customers opt in for quality as well. Aside from the carrot cake and the quality local organic ingredients they use, Carol and Sean know that people are attracted to the coffee house because they like that the owners are there most of the time and that they know their customers by name.

Kekuli Café

KEKULI CAFÉ

3041 Louie Drive, West Kelowna | 250-768-3555 | kekulicafe.com

Kekuli Café is the stop for some seriously amazing bannock (better than doughnuts!), also known as frybread, and organic coffee and espresso. While the bannock is a bit of an indulgence, I like that the menu has a healthy bent and there's an environmental business ethos. Owner SHARON BOND-HOGG (Nooaitch First Nation) is the driving force behind Kekuli Café, which is opening new horizons in local culinary options with saskatoon berry tea lemonade, saskatoon berry smoothies, and a wild smoked salmon egg "bannodict."

OKANAGAN STREET FOOD

812 Crowley Avenue, Kelowna | 778-478-0807 | okanaganstreetfood.com

NEIL SCHROETER, a Red Seal chef, has spent his fair share of a professional career working in fine dining and high-end restaurants across Canada. He was executive chef at the Delta Whistler Village Suites before heading up the kitchen at the Whistler Conference Centre and then moving to the Okanagan to serve as executive chef at the Cellar Door Bistro at Sumac Ridge Estate Winery for several years. In 2010, he struck out on his own, catching the food truck phenomenon early on. Mind you, Schroeter's Okanagan Street Food truck was where I'd go for a quart of exquisite veal stock as much as a fish taco on market days. Now Okanagan Street Food has a brick-and-mortar location on the industrial edge of downtown Kelowna. Schroeter has a loyal lunch clientele whom he knows by name, and they come for the quality comfort food like daily pasta specials, fresh cut fries with homemade blackberry ketchup or truffled mayo, or the epic pulled pork sandwich. There's also a busy catering arm to Okanagan Street Food, hence the "breakfast and lunch only" hours at the restaurant.

nch **11am - 3pm**

Soup 8oz $5 / 16 oz $7
ed with house cracker and fresh baguette
fresh sheet for today's selections

k cut fries $6
a Blackberry ketchup or truffled mayonnaise

ied salmon risotto fritters $9
e smoked salmon, rice, cream, parmesan, lemongrass and herbs
n-t lemongrass dipping sauce

ar salad $9
y romaine, house dressing, grana padano parmesan and herbed croutons
ed with house parmesan and rosemary cracker

h grilled chicken breast $13

kfast wrap $9
t bacon, egg, aged cheddar, and fresh salsa baked in a flour tortilla

es do not include tax

Lunch 11am -

Classic poutine $10
fresh cut fries, cheese curds, hot homemade gravy
with pulled pork, or local bacon $13

Veggie fries $11
fresh cut fries, cheese curds, caramelized onion, mushrooms, roa
hot homemade cheese sauce

Mac n cheese $11 (takes 20 minutes to bake)
housemade fresh penne, fresh cheese sauce baked with more che
with pulled pork or local bacon $14
with mushrooms, roast peppers and caramelized onion

Daily pasta $13
fresh housemade pasta with baguette
see fresh sheet for today's feature

prices do not include tax

Neil Schroeter

CODFATHERS SEAFOOD MARKET

2355 Gordon Drive, Kelowna | 250-763-3474 | codfathers.ca

When I have a seafood or fish question, I ask JONATHAN or ANNE-MARIE CROFTS. They're the husband-and-wife team behind Codfathers Seafood Market.

The Crofts grew up in Poole in the south of England. Jonathan's maternal great-grandfather and paternal grandfather were both fishmongers, and it was always Jonathan's dream to own his own fish shop. The Crofts arrived in Canada in 2002. Not being "big city people," they loved Kelowna's beauty and felt it was the perfect size for opportunity without the headaches and madness of too much urbanity. Soon after they arrived, they asked a friend where they could get good, fresh seafood. She directed them to Codfathers and casually noted that she'd heard the business was up for sale. The Crofts struck a deal with the owner and worked with him for six months as the sale went through. In February 2003, Jonathan and Anne-Marie became the new owners of Codfathers Seafood Market.

Every trip to Codfathers is also an education, as Jonathan is passionate about the sourcing, sustainability, and traceability of the seafood selection. "If I could get one message across, it's how important it is to know where your fish comes from and how it is produced," he says. "I find it so disappointing to see fish available that I know has been caught and produced at a huge social and environmental cost just because there's a demand for cheap protein here." Codfathers has greatly expanded my fish knowledge and palate in the past decade. Ask a question at the counter, and it might just be a marine biologist or a fishery technician answering back. Or leave the cooking up to Codfathers' café chef, ROSS DERRICK. Every product at Codfathers is either certified by Ocean Wise™, the Vancouver Aquarium assurance of an ocean-friendly seafood choice, or has been specifically selected by the team as the most sustainable option from small, artisanal fisheries.

Through the Crofts' constant efforts of education and instrumental

Anne-Marie and Jon Crofts, and kids

participation in everything from the Osoyoos Oyster Festival, to the Okanagan Nation Alliance's Okanagan sockeye fishery, to the Slow Food Thompson Okanagan convivium activities, they are making a huge impact on quality, ethical, and sustainable food in the region. They supply many of the valley's best fine dining restaurants and have a solid retail clientele at their shop and in-store restaurant in Kelowna. "In 2003, our sales were made up of about 10 to 12 varieties of fish. Now we regularly stock 40 to 50 types of fresh fish," says Jonathan. They also regularly carry a dozen varieties of fresh oysters as well as other seafood you won't find elsewhere: gooseneck barnacles, smelts, skate, and seasonal fresh BC spot prawns.

YOU MIGHT ALSO LIKE

LITTLE MISS CHIEF, for the wild, Pacific Ocean–caught smoked salmon, brined in organic Okanagan dry white wine for an interesting, delicious twist on cold-smoked salmon. Owner and CEO ELLEN MELCOSKY (Esketemc First Nation) is an inspiring business success story, with her smoked salmon distributed nationally and internationally. (2440 Old Okanagan Highway, West Kelowna, 250-768-6977, littlemisschief.com)

Scott Moran

SCOTT MORAN

Kelowna | 250-681-3431

"Weeds are technically wild herbs," SCOTT MORAN tells me, which meshes completely with my unkept and rather weedy garden. Moran grew up roasting foraged mushrooms over a campfire when other kids would be toasting marshmallows. (His dad, Larry Moran, has been rambling around BC and up to the Northwest Territories and the Yukon for decades, chasing morels after forest fires do their work.) In 2011, after a particularly good year of picking and selling mushrooms, Moran had enough money to visit his brother, Paul, who was building his culinary career in a kitchen in Paris. While there, Moran hopped over to the UK, where he got a job with Miles Irving, perhaps the most famous forager in Europe, who supplies Michelin-starred and fine dining restaurants. Under Irving's instruction, Moran learned about identifying and collecting over 100 different wild herbs and edibles there. After returning a year and half later, he found many of the same wild edibles growing in the central interior, and he now makes his living as a professional forager. Moran supplies some of the valley's top restaurants with items ranging from wild cattails to wild mustards and miner's lettuce. He also sells at the Kelowna Farmers' and Crafters' Market through Urban Harvest.

BC TREE FRUITS

1473 Water Street, Kelowna | 250-762-5571 | bctree.com

BC Tree Fruits is a packing and marketing co-operative owned by over 500 local farming families who grow varieties of apples, apricots, nectarines, peaches, cherries, prune plums, blueberries, and Coronation (table) grapes. It's been around since 1936, and you likely recognize the logo: a green apple leaf with red and white lettering at the centre. While I could write about many of BC Tree Fruits' interesting and talented orchardists, HANK MARKGRAF is my go-to guy for any questions about fruit in the valley.

As manager of growers' services for BC Tree Fruits, Markgraf's job is to translate the hard science of growing these fruits into the soft art of what the farmers do in the orchard. The valley's brain trust, he has a deep grasp of everything from irrigation best practices and pruning, to pest control, to the business of being a relatively small fruit-growing region on the world stage. Markgraf notes the Okanagan's ideal attributes for growing these fruits: the availability of fresh water that can be so readily recycled within the Okanagan watershed; the heat and low humidity, but with cool nights during harvest time to bring out the best colour and flavour in fruit; the soils and hill slopes that are so great for well-drained soil. The Okanagan, with its Canadian winters, also has less disease and pest pressure than many other global fruit-growing regions. However, due to the high land prices in the Okanagan, and the fact that BC Tree Fruits' growers pay their workers living wages, "our growers need to be pretty productive to make their orchards sustainable," says Markgraf.

This is why, he says, the Okanagan leads North America in high-density planting of apples, where the orchards feature tall, skinny trees compared to a traditional orchard where each hulking tree has a huge umbrella canopy. Trees are also planted more closely to one another in straight rows, like vineyards, where 1,200 to 1,500 trees per acre are the norm. (Early apple orchards were planted with 200 to 250 trees per

COURTESY OF BC TREE FRUITS / TIM KELLY BRANDFX

Darcel and Hank Markgraf, and dog Kylie

acre.) While it perhaps makes for less scenic orchards than a generation ago, high-density planting allows farmers to more than double their production and have greater quality control and much easier harvesting. Part of the sustainability aspect to growing fruit in the Okanagan is to make sure that growers can pick more easily and have a higher daily harvest, as they get paid by the weight of fruit they pick per day. "Every one of your apples is hand-picked," says Markgraf. "Each pear. Each peach."

DARCEL MARKGRAF, Hank's wife, works on the family farm and contributes to the marketing efforts of BC Tree Fruits as a freelance home economist. She's a staunch supporter of the home cook and has a very keen grip on how busy people need to make the most of any time in the kitchen. I look to her for tips on fruit recipes on the BC Tree Fruits website; one of my favourites is her spiced apple rings.

Jas Sanghera and Harkirat Sanghera

DON-O-RAY VEGETABLES

3443 Benvoulin Road, Kelowna | 250-860-2557 | donoray.com

There's something to be said for not fixing it if it's not broken. Don-O-Ray Vegetables is a farm, orchard, fruit stand, and market stop that has been around since 1960. And from the looks of it, it hasn't changed much in those decades. The very first time I met the farm manager, JAS SANGHERA, I was struck by his absolute love of growing field crops and fruit. He walked me through his rows of romaine, green cabbage, indigo-coloured cauliflower (purple vegetables are very in right now), golden beets, and Romanesco broccoli, which all belong in a Flemish still-life tableau. Farming isn't an easy life, and artisan farmers don't get rich at it. So it must be love. As the sign says, "Picked Fresh Daily." You can't improve on that.

YOU MIGHT ALSO LIKE

LITTLE CREEK DRESSING, for the excellent vinaigrettes that Donna Denison and Dale Zeich have been producing since 1995 from ingredients grown on their certified organic Kelowna farm. Look for them in most valley grocery stores. (778-478-1879, littlecreekdressing.com)

GATZKE ORCHARD

15690 Pelmewash Parkway, Oyama | 250-548-3444 | gatzkeorchard.com

The story goes that while coming out west, Leo Gatzke fell asleep and missed his intended train stop in Saskatchewan. He leapt out in Oyama and established a farm in 1929, and three generations later, ALAN GATZKE, his wife, INGRID GATZKE, and their two daughters live on and operate Gatzke Orchards. They grow and sell 50 to 60 ground crops organically (though not certified), and they cultivate 60 species of fruit trees, working toward organic certification. They make 5,000 to 7,000 pies a year, by hand, which are served at the farm or taken home by customers. And throughout the year, they sell over 80 value-added products like jams, preserves, and sauces that they make from farm produce. Gatzke Orchards hosts on-farm "GO Foodism" dinners (GO as in "go," but also as in the initials of Gatzke Orchard) featuring local chefs who showcase the farm's produce.

What I like most is how fearless Gatzke seems, or at least how he embraces challenge and strikes out in his own direction. Talking about the challenges of the 1980s and 1990s, when free trade flooded the market with tariff-free fruit, "it was sink or swim," he says. "It took us a few years to replant for things that we could sell direct to consumers." They planted a new orchard and started doing on-farm tours and offering meals for groups in the 1990s. They transitioned the farm's fruit stand into a café-restaurant. Then a bakery. Then a space for weddings. With each of these additions, he had to work to establish permits and change bylaws. Twenty-six thousand cars a day used to pass in front of the farm, but in 2014, the highway was rerouted, which reduced the daily drive-by traffic to 600 cars, dropping the business at the farm by half that summer. "There were challenges on the business side," Gatzke admits, "but the view from the deck on our café has improved." Now customers seek them out for the freshness and quality of their fruit and field crops—"the right people," as he says. The highway rerouting has also been good for Oyama as a whole, he says, since the new highway

Alan and Ingrid Gatzke

doesn't cut the town in half, which will make it a greater community than it would have been otherwise.

"There hasn't been a model that I've followed," Alan reflects. "It's been a recipe that I wrote and tried to make happen." He even served two terms on the local city council to bring the bylaws into line with the needs of agritourism. I love that he's not bitter at the uphill battle. And he's thrilled that the changes are now starting to foster a culinary movement in Oyama. "The town is behind the times, in that there are just a couple of businesses here, but in terms of having all the ingredients, the place is very rich."

Curtis Stone

GREEN CITY ACRES

1241 Lawson Avenue, Kelowna (no on-site sales) | 250-899-4835 | greencityacres.com

I came upon CURTIS STONE in 2010, when I was writing my first book, *Food and the City*, which looked at urban farmers and urban agriculture models around the world. Stone was a first-year novice farmer who was using a new urban-farming model of borrowing people's front lawns, ripping them up, and planting them with market crops to sell at farmers' markets and to restaurants. That first year, he grew 22,700 kilograms (50,000 pounds) of fresh leafy greens and other veggies on less than an acre of borrowed land in Kelowna. He accomplished all this with a $7,000 investment, using a bicycle to pull his rototiller around to the various garden plots, to take his market greens to the Kelowna Farmers' and Crafters' Market and to restaurant clients, and to pick up compost. And he made a $22,000 profit.

Five years later, Green City Acres is thriving. With only one other employee, Stone grows only the 15 crops that have proven to be his best-sellers over the past few years, and he sells only to Kelowna's best restaurants and at his market booth. Stone's multi-location farm amounts to about one-third of an acre on land borrowed from various homeowners. In exchange for rent, Stone gives them a basket of produce every week of the growing season. While the learning curve was steep, Stone now makes an impressive $80,000 to $100,000 per season. During the winter season (November to the end of March), he is an in-demand public speaker and urban-farming educator throughout the US, Canada, and Mexico. He's also the author of *The Urban Farmer: Growing Food for Profit on Leased and Borrowed Land* (New Society Publishers, 2015).

HILLCREST FARM MARKET

700 Highway 33 East, Kelowna | 250-765-8000 | hillcrestfarmmarket.com

In 1914, Bhagu Singh and a friend walked from Vancouver to Kelowna on a rumour that good agricultural land was to be found in the Okanagan. Prevented like many Indo-Canadians from owning land at the time, Singh crop-shared, saved money, and had another farmer purchase land for him. When the laws changed to allow him to legally own land, the deal was fortunately honoured and the beautiful, sprawling 100-acre orchard is still in the family, three generations later.

CHANCHAL AND BARBARA BAL (the latter is Bhagu Singh's grand-daughter) and their four children have invested heavily in an on-farm packing plant, direct-to-consumer facilities like the farm market and café, and even four lovely B&B rooms above the market and café in the past few years. I've been known to drive all the way to Kelowna just for Barbara Bal's incredibly lacy pakora with onions, spinach, and potatoes at the café and to buy other field veg and fruit from the farm. And what started out as an after-school snack in the Bal household, butter chicken pizza, is now a signature menu item. A retail fresh market sells the farm's preserves, juices, many varieties of peppers, tomatoes, broccoli, lettuce, eggplant, and, of course, tree fruits. SUKHPAUL BAL (eldest son of Chanchal and Barbara) manages the farming operations. Hillcrest grows six varieties of cherries, and their quality attracts the attention of international buyers who pay top dollar for them all over the world. But we can buy them right where they're picked.

COURTESY OF HILLCREST FARM MARKET

From left to right: Varinder Bal, Sukhpaul Bal, (Archer), Mandeep Bal, Daljit Bal, Dilraj Bal, Chanchal Bal, Barbara Bal, Davinder Sangha, and Kavraj Sangha

THE HOMESTEAD ORGANIC FARM

4855 MacKinnon Road, Peachland | 250-767-6636 | thehomesteadorganicfarm.ca

I came to know JORDAN MARR through his thoughtful podcasts and blog (theruminant.ca), which are aimed at young farmers finding their way in sustainable, quality-driven agriculture. But his actual job is as a market gardener and farm manager on a soaring 25-acre piece of forest and farmland that looks out over Okanagan Lake from above Trepanier Bench, about 210 metres (700 feet) from where the lake bends across from Okanagan Mountain Park. The view, he admits, is a nice perk of the job.

On January 1, 2011, Marr and his then girlfriend, now wife, Vanessa Samur, arrived at the Homestead, Joe and Jessica Klein's organic farm, allowing the Kleins to back off and enjoy some travel after 35 years of hard work. Marr and Samur had apprenticed on a farm that specialized in high-quality salad greens, and they brought their skills to bear at the Homestead. Though they planned to farm together, Samur now works off-farm as a licensed midwife, which is a practical way to diversify their income as a couple. Marr leases two acres from the Kleins for his Community Supported Agriculture (CSA) program and market garden and manages the bulk of the farming operations; Joe Klein continues to actively manage the organic hay production.

Marr's CSA program dictates that he grow a wide variety of crops, but he is focusing more and more on greens and edible flowers for his chef customers. At the peak of variety, his mixed salad bag might include over 20 different greens, like Persian cress, crinkly cress, and Malabar spinach, as well as nasturtium leaves and flowers or calendula petals. He admits that this level of variety in the greens is much more work than the standard spring mix, as the harvest of some varieties of flowers or greens is out of synch with others, yet he feels the extra work is worth it. He checks in with his chefs every couple of weeks to make sure that the quality of the product is where it needs to be. He also allows a "no

Jordan Marr

commitment" one-time purchase option from his CSA, because he likes the challenge of having to win a customer each and every time they buy from him.

As for being a "landless farmer" who is currently leasing, Marr is inspired by that challenge too. Rather than being dissuaded by the high price in the Okanagan agriculture land game, part of his business plan is to eventually own his own farm. "As I grow the business, it doesn't seem impossible," he says—another reason for hope that the local food scene will continue to mature and flourish.

Jennay Oliver

PAYNTER'S FRUIT MARKET

3687 Paynter Road, West Kelowna | 250-768-7313 | payntersfruitmarket.ca

On July 7, 1951, Henry Paynter wrote in his diary: "Sold our first cherries on the side of the road." Paynter's Fruit Stand in Westbank was born. In 2013, JENNAY OLIVER, granddaughter of Henry and Sheila Paynter, won Young Entrepreneur of the Year from the Westbank/West Kelowna Chamber of Commerce for the thriving Paynter's Fruit Market over which she now presides.

Cherries, apricots, peaches, plums, apples, and pears are Paynter's Fruit Market's specialty. The orchard is mere steps from the fruit stand, offering customers the option of U-pick or purchasing Paynter's fruit and veg at the in-store market. In the past few years, Paynter's has diversified into field crops—tomatoes, cucumbers, peppers, eggplant, squash, herbs, chard, kale, zucchini, and more—grown with minimal sprays and using only organic methods like oils and soaps to control pests. Homestead Organics vegetables are also available through Paynter's, as are a collection of quality local products like Little Creek Dressings, Fieldstone Organics' whole grains and seeds, Ogopogo Hot Sauce, Summerland Sweets fruit syrups and jams, Caramoomel, and various local honeys.

Henry Paynter lived to the age of 98; his wife Sheila, now in her mid-90s, still shows up to lend a hand in the orchard and at the fruit stand. Not only does she know her way around a fruit orchard, she has authored three books: *First Time Around* (1991), about the 270-kilometre (170-mile), 24-day walk she did around Okanagan Lake when she was 70; *Reflections on the Lake* (1994), about her paddle around the perimeter of the lake; and *Okanagan Golf: Points of View* (1996). Sheila continues to write a monthly column for *Westside Weekly*, the local newspaper.

SPROULE & SONS FARM

4590 Allison Road, Oyama | 250-548-3387 | sproulesredbarn.com

Established in 1946, Sproule & Sons Farm sits on rolling hills with a view of Kalamalka Lake that you could lose yourself in all day long. NEIL SPROULE had the luck to grow up on this piece of land, working alongside his parents in the orchard. In 1992, Neil and his wife, JACQUI, bought the property and decided to turn it into a certified organic farm "for health reasons and for a better environment," says Neil. This type of land stewardship comes with a lot more work year-round compared to shortcuts with synthetic fertilizers and pesticides, but the Sproules were also raising their young family on the farm.

Manure composts over several weeks in the winter. Once "cured," the nutrient-rich compost is spread around the orchard. Pruning is another winter and early spring task. As soon as the blossoms appear, it's time to bring in the beehives for pollination. The fruit is then thinned and watched carefully for ripeness.

Sproule's has a broad selection of varieties within each fruit they grow. I'm finding organic cherries harder and harder to come by as they either get shipped immediately for export or are difficult to grow in the first place due to pest issues. So Sproule's is a bonanza with its Lambert, Rainier, Lapin, Skeena, and Sweetheart varieties. Sproule's also makes a certified organic cherry juice so good, it's obscene. The orchard contains interesting varieties of peaches, such as the white-fleshed Raritan Rose and the Canadian Harvest, among others. All fruit is grown and packed on the farm—cherries, apricots, nectarines, grapes, peaches, plums, and apples—and is available for sale in the red barn on the property or at farmers' markets in Kelowna, Vernon, Salmon Arm, and Nakusp.

Jacqui and Neil Sproule

Sonia Sandhu, and daughter

SUN CITY CHERRIES

4759 Lakeshore Road, Kelowna | 250-764-1872

This is another multi-generational Kelowna orcharding family business. SONIA SANDHU manages the large operation, running crews of pickers, sorters, and packers 24 hours a day during cherry harvest season. It's an intense couple of months when the entire year's income rests on getting their incredible cherries largely to lucrative foreign markets.

Sandhu grew up in the business, developing stamina and focus early on and learning that hard work was simply part of the job. (In one sense, it's a shame about all the exports, but I'm glad these farming families have good markets for their fruit. And maybe it's time we started valuing our quality fruit more than we do. Can you really put a price on the two weeks of intense perfection when cherries have so much inky juice that it seems impossible for their soft skins to hold it all in?)

Sun City Cherries is open from the end of June to the end of October, with U-pick from mid-July to mid-August. The fruit stand also sells honey, homemade jams, fresh field vegetables, and other fruit.

KNIFEWEAR

2983 Pandosy Street, Kelowna | 778-478-0331 | knifewear.com

Had it not been for the arrival of Knifewear in Kelowna and my husband's insistence that money spent on good kitchen knives is money well spent, I would never have known the pleasure of hand-forged Japanese steel in my hands. And that would have been a shame. We now own several knives from Knifewear, and I assure you they are worth every penny. I happily spend hours paring apples from our backyard Gala tree with my lovely sickle-shaped, two-and-a-half-inch Classic Bird's Beak Shun knife, while my husband loves chopping and dicing with his eight-inch Konosuke Mirror knife.

Knifewear began when Kevin Kent was working as a chef in the UK and selling Japanese-made knives out of a backpack on the side. Kent returned to Canada and opened Knifewear in Calgary in 2007, and a business was born. He opened Knifewear Kelowna in 2012, then shops in Ottawa and Edmonton in 2013. Kent now travels to Japan frequently to meet with and buy directly from his network of Japanese craftsmen, many of whom descend from sword-making families from the Samurai era.

MARK PUTTICK manages Knifewear Kelowna, a narrow shop filled with many irresistible hand-forged knives. Knifewear Kelowna's in-store Chef Wall of Fame features pretty much every Okanagan chef posing with their beloved Japanese steel. Knifewear also sells sharpening stones, honing tools, foodie mags, cookbooks, cutting boards, and other goodies. And for guys who are into straight-razor shaving, Knifewear's got you covered too.

Let's just admit it, there's something super-sexy about these beautiful knives, and pleasure is an important ingredient in any good cooking. Knifewear is a hub for the valley's culinary industry, and there's a pretty good chance that you'll bump into a chef or two when they come in to sharpen a knife or to browse the cookbooks and magazines and dream of the next knife to add to their roll.

Mark Puttick

Andrea and Dave McFadden

OKANAGAN LAVENDER AND HERB FARM

4380 Takla Road, Kelowna | 250-764-7795 | okanaganlavender.com

I take friends and visitors to the Okanagan Lavender and Herb Farm because you just can't beat the wow factor of their indigo and pink waves of lavender fields, photo-perfect rose bushes, and multi-sensory culinary herb gardens. In 1994, ANDREA AND DAVE MCFADDEN planted a test plot of lavender on their farm, which they bought from Andrea's father, Dick Stewart, an orchardist and early wine pioneer who planted the property with apples beginning in the 1950s. (Dick Stewart also planted wine grapes on a property in West Kelowna, now Quails' Gate Estate Winery.) "I'd read a newspaper article in the *Guardian* about the disappearing lavender fields in Provence," says Andrea, explaining the pest problem in the south of France that threatens the region's iconic lavender industry. Coming from a winemaking family, Andrea wondered if lavender would be free of this disease in North America, similar to how the global wine industry was saved from phylloxera thanks to North American grape rootstock.

The lavender grew beautifully, and the McFaddens converted an old pickers' cottage into a retail shop. They gradually expanded the lavender plantings, adding other flowers and culinary herbs—basil, lemon balm, summer and winter savory, spearmint, sage, oregano, rosemary, and thyme. Now it's a haven for garden enthusiasts as well as a place to pick up Okanagan aromatherapy products (distilled on-farm), soaps, and herb mixes. Signature products are the house-distilled lavender essential oils and rosewater, which is excellent in rice pudding, yogurt mousse, or even butter cookies.

SUNSHINE FARM

2225 Saucier Road, Kelowna (no on-farm sales) | 250-448-1826 | sunshinefarm.net

I consider Sunshine Farm as a living food bank and an heirloom food sanctuary, the kind of farm that may be the last good hope for flavour and variety in our not-so-distant future of food. Sunshine Farm is a 12-and-a-half-acre property in Southeast Kelowna, where JON AND SHER ALCOCK have been saving open-pollinated, organic vegetable, lettuce, and herb seeds, growing heirloom, certified organic market produce, and providing vocational services for adults with developmental disabilities through Community Living BC.

I've had the pleasure of visiting Sunshine Farm a few times, first with chef Rod Butters of RauDZ Regional Table, who is a long-time customer of their outstanding market produce. The farm is known for its especially flavourful heirloom tomatoes and carrots. Jon explains that the sandy loam soil is thanks to glacial Lake Penticton, which stretched from the North to the South Okanagan over 12,000 years ago. When the lake drained, the mineral, silts, and clay deposits in Southeast Kelowna created ideal growing conditions for plants that take on the minerality of the soil, like tomatoes, potatoes, carrots, turnips, and salsify.

Aside from market produce, which is for sale at the Kelowna Farmers' and Crafters' Market twice a week, Sunshine Farm's seed catalogue is an important link in the local food chain, keeping local, open-pollinated, organic seeds in circulation and available to other market gardeners and individuals, as do seed swaps and farmers' markets. International seed companies don't give a hoot about the really great variety of carrot that grows splendidly in the Okanagan, because it's such a small part of the much more profitable market. A few holdouts, like the Alcocks, are doing their part in a network of independent seed farms in Canada that need to be supported. Seed farms like Sunshine are the only thing between me and a table without purple dragon carrots, Whangaparaoa Crown pumpkin, Rousanne Violette carrots, and Bianca a Uovo eggplant, if you catch my drift.

PHOTO BY JASMIN DOSANJ

Sher and Jon Alcock

Michael Daley

BC TREE FRUITS CIDER COMPANY

880 Vaughan Avenue, Kelowna | 250-979-2629 | bctreefruitscider.com

After 80 years in the growing, picking, packing, shipping, and marketing business, BC Tree Fruits, the co-operative of 500 orchards in the valley, launched itself into the craft cider business. Given its access to BC-grown apples, it just made sense to catch the cider boom and give its grower members a share in the benefits that a value-added product like cider can offer.

In June 2015, the Kelowna tasting lounge opened and the all-apple Broken Ladder Cider was rolled out both on tap and in cans. The top-secret cider recipe, a blend of six Okanagan-grown apple varieties, was developed by BERTUS ALBERTYN, winemaker at Burrowing Owl Estate Winery and Albertyn's own Maverick Estate Winery, in collaboration with MICHAEL DALEY, BC Tree Fruit Cider Company project manager. It's a straw-coloured, modern-style cider that has just enough—but not too much—sweetness.

EAST KELOWNA CIDER CO.

2960 McCullough Road, Kelowna | 250-860-3610 | eastkelownacider.com

Back when the Okanagan was the apple basket of Canada, and even the world, East Kelowna was covered by large, sprawling orchards, and Charles Ross bought a 20-acre orchard here in 1942. It was planted mostly with apples, but there was a small cherry orchard as well. Two generations later, DAVE ROSS (JR.) and his wife, THERESSA, manage the family homestead. They've diversified to include some peaches, pears, and plums along with the cherries for direct-to-consumer sales on-farm. But the main crop is still apple. They grow seven varieties of apples and harvest about 136,000 kilograms (300,000 pounds) per year. Most of the crop is sold privately, but a small portion is kept for the East Kelowna Cider Company, the Okanagan's first land-based, or estate, cidery, which they established in 1995.

Their signature product is the Ross Winter Burn, a limited-edition iced cider, but they also produce the intriguing Ross Icy Peach and Ross Logger Cider, the latter a hard cider that shares flavour profiles with a lager beer. The view from the patio can't be beat, especially in the heat of the summer while savouring an apple gelato made from Ross apple cider.

Dave Ross Jr. and Theressa Ross with son and dog

COURTESY OF JIRI BAKALA / MEADOW VISTA HONEY WINES

Judie Barta

MEADOW VISTA HONEY WINES

3975 June Springs Road, Kelowna | 250-862-2337 | meadowvista.ca

JUDIE BARTA is a self-described serial entrepreneur. She moved to the Okanagan in 1993 and was a sales representative for Sumac Ridge wines back in the early days when there were only 16 licensed wineries in the valley. Then she opened a spa and became a massage therapist and wellness expert. A chance conversation about mead—essentially fermented honey—with a local wine consultant left her with the idea to make mead by employing winemaking techniques rather than traditional meadmaking methods. In 2009, she began Meadow Vista, specifically using the term *honey wines* to acknowledge that she'd be making wines from honey using skills she had picked up from the grape-wine industry.

"Instead of terroir, I talk about nectar," says Barta when welcoming new customers to her serene tasting room on a beautiful acreage in Southeast Kelowna. "And instead of varietals, I talk about style," she adds, because the main ingredient, honey, doesn't change. The winemaker's art comes in with the various fermentation techniques and knowing which other ingredients to blend in. Her Joy was the first honey wine in Canada to employ the *méthode traditionnelle*, the classic double-fermentation technique to create sparkling wine. Cloud Horse is a surprisingly dry honey wine, which is something that Pinot Gris drinkers tend to appreciate. Bliss is also a sparkling honey wine, but with a dash of Okanagan cherry juice for a beautiful rose-coloured patio sipper. Mabon is blended with cardamom, coriander, cinnamon, and nutmeg—Thanksgiving dinner in a bottle, if you like, good as a mulled wine or with pumpkin pie. Ostara blends Okanagan Pinot Gris with honey wine for some tropical fruit and citrus aromas. When available, Meadow Vista Libra is a sweet, dessert fruit and honey wine made from Okanagan apricots. Barta knows that she's got an uphill battle to win over converts, but she's on her way. Maybe even with me.

TREE BREWING BEER INSTITUTE

1346 Water Street, Kelowna | 778-484-0306 | treebrewingbeerinstitute.com

In 1995, Tree Brewing opened in Kelowna and made small-batch beers in flavour-forward styles that probably woke up a few taste buds in the valley. The focus was on the basic ingredients of malted barley, hops, and water. The first keg of Tree Beer, its amber ale, was sold in 1996 to a restaurant called Water Street Grill in downtown Kelowna. That beer, now called Thirsty Beaver Amber Ale, is still a steady seller for Tree, and the new Tree Brewing Beer Institute opened in the summer of 2014 in the location that Water Street Grill once occupied.

DAVE GOKIERT has been the brewmaster at Tree Brewing since 2014; he's worked there, however, since 1997. He began with the humble jobs, working and learning from the brewmasters who came before him. He jokes that he's merely stubborn and stayed as others moved on, but his brewing career has been more deliberate than his light demeanour suggests. Born and raised in Westlock, Alberta, Gokiert received a Bachelor of Science in Chemistry at the University of Alberta because he knew he wanted to go into brewing and figured that would give him the knowledge base required for the industry. The early days in craft brewing in the Okanagan, as elsewhere in the West, seem like a lifetime ago. "Brewers were not as adventurous and drinkers were not as adventurous," says Gokiert. "Now people really know their styles, their hops. They want to know the IBU and the ABV of each beer," he says—beer talk that refers to the International Bittering Units scale and the Alcohol by Volume calculation.

Gokiert is enjoying the creative licence, but now as the wise old man in the brew space, his job is to slow down the younger employees. The first step is to make an excellent liquid before adding the other layers on top, balancing the sweetness of the malt with the hops, the body, and the alcohol. This is where his chemistry training really kicks in. "It's not about regurgitating a recipe. I'm in control of the hops, the yeast, the water." He loves the quality of Okanagan lake water, which is cold, deep

Dave Gokiert

(for good consistency year-round), and has "maybe a little bit of Ogopogo," he laughs, referring to the Okanagan's own mythical lake creature.

The Beer Institute is not only a working brewery, but also a tasting lounge with delicious menu items like pretzels, which incorporate spent grains from the brewing process and are served with ale honey mustard. Patrons can order tasting flights, growler refills, cask ales, and an ever-rotating selection of tank-to-tap craft beer. Oh, and a spicy housemade rootbeer for the non-drinkers and minors.

URBAN DISTILLERIES

325 Bay Avenue, Kelowna | 778-478-0939 | urbandistilleries.ca

Lavender is a tricky botanical. Too much and it's all you taste. But just enough to be "barely there" and it becomes intriguing. That's what I love about Urban Distilleries' Spirit Bear Gin. The subtle hints of local lavender and apples among the 10 different botanicals in this recipe make it a wonderfully distinctive Okanagan spirit. More specifically, it makes an excellent gin and tonic. Urban Distilleries' Spirit Bear line includes an exceptionally clean vodka as well as an espresso-infused version made from the certified organic beans of Kelowna's Cherry Hill Coffee, roasted in small batches by hand in a rebuilt 1960s Vittoria roaster.

The man behind the alchemy is MIKE URBAN, an electronics engineer by trade who saw the global winds of outsourcing blowing his career options overseas to Asia. Already a hobby distiller, he was deeply inspired by a trip to a Cognac house in France, which put the wheels in motion to open his own craft distillery in October 2010. In those days, he was allowed to locate only in an industrial zone, and now he admits that it's too expensive to move—though Urban Distilleries is just a few blocks away from Kelowna's historic downtown district.

Building a reputation for excellent clear spirits—his vodkas and gin—Urban also launched BC's first (and Canada's third) single malt whisky a few years ago, complete with a small chip of oak in each bottle that allows the whisky to continue to acquire oak-aging in-bottle. Urban Distilleries also has a Grappa Moscato, a clear *digestivo* made from the skins, seeds, pulp, and stems left over from the winemaking process. And as the name suggests, this grappa is made with the pomace of Moscato grapes, which are fragrant and floral. And Urban put up his first batch of rye whisky in 2015, but we'll have to wait until 2018 for a nip of that.

Urban is now on a mission to train others who want to get into the craft distillery game. His five-day hands-on workshops promise everything

Mike Urban

you need to learn about starting a distillery, from the basics of fermentation and distilling using the on-site stills to navigating the bureaucracy and regulations of starting your own craft distillery. Not surprisingly, given the recent interest in distilling, Urban's courses are always full.

YOU MIGHT ALSO LIKE

DOUBLE CROSS CIDERY, for the outstanding iced ciders that Indira and Ravi Pannu still make after buying Glenn and Loretta Cross's orchard and Function-Junction apple juice line in 2015. My favorite is Pink Lady Iced Cider. (811 Highway 33 East, Kelowna, 250-863-8011: Indira, 250-863-0757: Ravi, function-junction.ca/double_cross_cidery.html)

WARDS CIDERY, for a line of traditional ciders from European cider apples that were planted in the 1920s on the orchard that is still in the Turton-Ward family. (2287 Ward Road, Kelowna, 250-215-1331, wardshardcider.com)

ROD BUTTERS

Micro Bar Bites | 1500 Water Street, Kelowna | 778-484-3500 | microkelowna.com

RauDZ Regional Table | 1560 Water Street, Kelowna | 250-868-8805 | raudz.com

ROD BUTTERS was a "pretty good ball player," he admits, having been offered a baseball scholarship at a US university. An arm injury forced a shift toward cooking, however, which was also a passion. He worked his way through kitchens at the Four Seasons Toronto and Vancouver, among others. By the time he was in his early 30s, he was hired as the chef de cuisine at the Pointe, the restaurant at the newly opened Wickaninnish Inn in Tofino, and established himself as one of the country's most exciting chefs and "the Wick" as one of Canada's top dining destinations.

The demands of the job took their toll, however, and Butters and AUDREY SURRAO (formerly married, they are still business partners and co-owners of RauDZ and Micro Bar Bites) went off on a 16-month globe-trotting adventure. Butters had standing job offers waiting for him when they returned to Canada in 2000. However, they felt it was time to work for themselves. The Okanagan, and Kelowna in particular, caught their attention with its burgeoning wine industry and established agricultural base. They opened Fresco in downtown Kelowna in 2001.

I was lucky enough to dine at Fresco not long after it opened, and every mouthful is deeply etched in my brain's catalogue of taste memories. I was on a press trip, and though I was rather green as a food writer, I could recognize an important meal when I tasted one. All these years later, I can still conjure up the remarkable freshness of the newly picked peas that were the supreme essence of a satiny soup topped with a dollop of crème fraîche and a sprig of fresh dill that started our dinner. I remember Butters talking about the local farmers who supplied the restaurant back when fine dining in just about every white tablecloth dining room from New York to Vancouver was epitomized by a thick slab

Rod Butters, Audrey Surrao

of Chilean sea bass on a bed of French lentils. Fresco's wine list also included Canadian wines alongside the Bordeaux and Napa selections. Fresco was the most exciting dining room in Kelowna, and it remained the reservation "get" for several years.

In a surprise move and despite having "their best year to date" in 2008, Butters and Surrao announced they'd be closing Fresco after New Year's Eve. They somehow knew that fine dining was waning and that diners were looking for less formality and more playfulness in their dining experience. They reopened with a radically new concept: RauDZ Regional Table, a hyper-local farm-to-table menu with an open kitchen, a no-reservations policy, and a 125-year-old reclaimed pine communal longtable. Butters boasted a dizzying roster of some 150 small, regional suppliers for the menu. Large black and white photos of farmer Jon Alcock of Sunshine Farm, Monika Walker of Okanagan Grocery Artisan Breads, and pioneering winemaker Howard Soon of Sandhill Estate Vineyard were hung as artwork on the heritage red-brick walls. Even the drinks menu walked the talk. Gerry Jobe (see page 144) was anointed as RauDZ's "liquid chef," and the field-to-glass concept and Okanagan cocktail movement were born.

Brock Bowes, Robyn Sigurdson

In 2013, Butters and Surrao opened the aptly named Micro Bar Bites. At 900 square feet, it's indeed a cozy wine bar with a small-bites tapas menu. Now Butters is mentoring the next generation of chefs, promoting talented cooks to take leadership roles, such as his current chefs de cuisine, BROCK BOWES and ROBYN SIGURDSON, along with EVELYNN TAKOFF (see page 159).

OKANAGAN CHEFS ASSOCIATION

okanaganchefs.com

Long before I moved to the Okanagan, I was aware of the Okanagan Chefs Association. Each province or region in Canada has an association that is part of the Canadian Culinary Federation, a member of the World Association of Chefs' Societies. At the local level, this is a volunteer organization of Okanagan chefs, culinary student members, and associate members (such as food writers) who are involved in the industry.

At about 200 members strong, the Okanagan Chefs Association is one of the most vibrant chefs associations in the country. Monthly meetings (10 per year) draw 60 to 80 members who eat together and discuss and celebrate their various professional and volunteer efforts. They volunteer an extradordinary amount of personal time to support major community events like the Canadian Cancer Society's annual fundraiser, the Daffodil Ball, as well as major fundraisers for Kelowna General Hospital and the Nature Trust of British Columbia. They also fundraise to support the professional development of their junior chef members, enabling them to hold intensive practice sessions and travel to national and international culinary competitions. The Okanagan Chefs Association is the heartbeat of professional cooking in the valley, and the boundless energy and ambition of its members have been a huge influence on the food and wine community here.

BERNARD CASAVANT

Okanagan College Food, Wine, and Tourism Programming

1000 KLO Road, Kelowna | okanagan.bc.ca/FWT

Chef BERNARD CASAVANT's name surfaces in many discussions I have with chefs and farmers in the valley. It's hard to sum up the influence he's had on the culinary scene in the Okanagan, other than to say that so many of the chefs running their own kitchens here these days started out under the wing of the man many simply call Chef Bernard.

Casavant knew his calling was cooking by high school. He signed up for every home economics class available, and he didn't mind being the only male in the classroom. After high school, he enrolled in the culinary arts program at Malaspina College (now known as Vancouver Island University), and graduated in 1976. He worked his way up through the ranks in kitchens across the West and became the fine dining chef at Vancouver's Expo '86. In 1989, he was the opening chef at Fairmont Chateau Whistler; Rod Butters was his sous-chef. In 1991, he was chosen to represent Canada at a prestigious international cooking competition, the Bocuse d'Or. Casavant continued at the Chateau Whistler until 1996, when he opened and ran his own café in the village. There he remained until 2006, when on a trip to the Okanagan to visit Butters and Audrey Surrao, Casavant fell for the potential of the region. He and his family moved to the South Okanagan, and this is when I first met him, as the executive chef at the Sonora Room at Burrowing Owl Estate Winery.

A founding member of FarmFolk CityFolk in Vancouver and involved in creating Whistler's first farmers' market, Casavant fully embraced and supported local farmers by putting the best of their products on his menus at the Sonora Room, the Watermark Beach Resort in Osoyoos, and the Manteo Resort's Smack DAB craft beer bistro in Kelowna. In 2008, his colleagues recognized his contributions to their profession by inducting him into the BC Restaurant Hall of Fame. A few years back,

Bernard Casavant

Casavant "retired," but he seems busier than ever with the restaurant consulting business he runs with his wife and long-time business partner, Bonnie Casavant. He's also currently leading the next generation of chefs as manager of culinary arts at Okanagan College's Centre for Food, Wine, and Tourism, and he continues to be a tireless behind-the-scenes mentor as the president of the Okanagan Chefs Association.

PHOTO BY JASMIN DOSANJ. COURTESY OF POPPADOMS—TASTE INDIA!

Aman, Jas, and Jasmin Dosanj

DOSANJ FAMILY

Poppadoms–Taste India! | 948 McCurdy Road, Kelowna | 778-753-5563 | poppadoms.ca

What's a young English footballer to do after playing goalkeeper for the national under-16 team and then signing with Arsenal Ladies? AMAN DOSANJ is nothing short of an overachiever, so when her professional sporting career ended early with a knee injury, she went off to the US on a university scholarship.

When the Dosanj family looked at Canada to start a new adventure, they crossed the pond and picked Kelowna to open a new kind of Indian restaurant. Poppadoms–Taste India! is regional Indian cuisine by way of the UK, so it has a global vibe while being fiercely loyal to local raw ingredients and wines. The restaurant has an unlikely location—a mall just off the main Kelowna thoroughfare of Harvey Avenue as it heads north of the city—for its level of culinary sophistication and worldliness. In other words, it's well worth seeking out.

Aman is a self-taught chef who began by learning the homespun East Indian techniques and flavours from her mother, JAS DOSANJ. Sister JASMIN is WSET (Wine and Spirit Education Trust) certified and runs the restaurant's wine program and the floor. Brother HARRY creates incredible cocktails with his housemade syrups, botanicals, and creative takes on East meets West at the bar. (Harry is an active member of the #okanagancocktailmovement and he pops up behind various bars in the valley.)

The Dosanjs just keep gaining respect for their tireless work ethic and endless culinary curiosity—clearly a family trait. They spend days off picking up new knowledge and ideas in other chefs' kitchens, roaming up and down the valley to eat at colleagues' restaurants, and participating in events through the Okanagan Chefs Association.

MARK FILATOW

Waterfront Wines | 1180 Sunset Drive, Kelowna

250-979-1222 | waterfrontrestaurant.ca

MARK FILATOW has one of the best wine-and-food-pairing palates I know. Each time I experience his food, whether at his restaurant, Waterfront Wines, in downtown Kelowna or at a special event at an Okanagan winery, my food and wine education leaps forward in the most pleasurable way. Filatow is one of the few chef-sommeliers in Canada, and he's brilliant at articulating how he puts together the various elements in his food with a particular wine—not that his food needs any interpretation. His creations are uncluttered and elegant, but tend to include a memorable twist that sheds new light on what you think you already know. He's also a pioneer of the local food movement in the valley and continues to be a leader in bringing the region's full culinary potential to the plate.

Filatow grew up in Mississauga but spent lots of time on his grandparents' acreage. His dad used to fix machinery for German butchers and bakers and was often paid in combinations of cash and blood sausage. He says that the smell of a smokehouse takes him right back to his childhood every time. He began cooking early, at the age of 16. Eventually he wanted to formalize his training, so he studied at Dubrulle International Culinary & Hotel Institute (now the Art Institute of Vancouver). After paying off culinary school by cooking in tree-planting camps (lucky tree planters!), Filatow landed a job with Rod Butters at the Wickaninnish Inn in Tofino. "It was supposed to be for three months, but I stayed for two years," says Filatow. He then cooked at Bishop's, another legendary West Coast restaurant, where he got very interested in wine education and quietly observed chef-proprietor John Bishop's management skills. He followed this with a stint at Diva at the Met in Vancouver before being lured to the Okanagan in 2001, again by Butters and Audrey Surrao, who were opening their own restaurant, Fresco, in downtown Kelowna. Filatow commuted to Vancouver on the weekends

Mark Filatow

to train as a sommelier while cooking at Fresco five nights a week. He built the wine program at Fresco and was the sous-chef for the first three years. He met and connected with local farmers who were thrilled to find that fine dining chefs were finally interested in quality local ingredients. Filatow finally took the opportunity to run his own kitchen when he signed on as executive chef at Waterfront Wines. Less than two years later, he was a partner in the business.

In 2012, Filatow, as chef at Waterfront Wines, won Gold Medal Plates, an intense national culinary competition in which regional winners from across Canada get a list of available ingredients and a wine pairing just hours before putting together a complex dish that is tasted and judged by some of Canada's top restaurant critics. Filatow still continues to create some of the most exciting food in the valley with the help of his capable kitchen brigade of sous-chefs at Waterfront, Nelson Daniels and Danny Tipper, as well as catering chef Graham Momer. Filatow also generously mentors other young chefs, colleagues, and culinary students at Okanagan College.

COURTESY OF MANTEO RESORT WATERFRONT HOTEL & VILLAS / SMACK DAB

Brad Horen

BRAD HOREN

Manteo Resort Waterfront Hotel & Villas | 3762 Lakeshore Road, Kelowna

250-860-1011 | manteo.com

Smack DAB | 250-860-4488 | smackdabmanteo.com

BRAD HOREN credits his grandmother and mother for his interest in cooking. "There was always something interesting going on in the kitchen," he says. Horen attended the culinary arts program at the Northern Alberta Institute of Technology in Edmonton, and right away he exhibited both culinary passion and endurance, working in the kitchen of the Shaw Conference Centre and being chosen as a member of Culinary Team Alberta. In 2002, Horen and team won what is known as the World Cup at a major international culinary competition in Luxembourg. Horen would go on to be captain of the much-medalled Culinary Team Alberta from 2008 to 2012.

Horen then left for Calgary, working first at the Westin and then as the executive chef at Catch, a well-regarded seafood restaurant opened by chef Michael Noble, for four years. He then headed up the kitchen at Laurel Point in Victoria and opened the Ottawa Convention Centre before moving to Kelowna. Now as the executive chef at the Manteo Resort Waterfront Hotel & Villas, with its Smack DAB wood-fired pizza and local craft brew, Horen finds inspiration from foraging trips in the valley for pine, morel, and oyster mushrooms. He has a light touch in the kitchen, letting quality ingredients take centre stage and patiently instructing his kitchen team on how to "treat these raw materials with care and respect after someone produces them so carefully."

GERRY JOBE

Niche Cocktails | Kelowna | 250-868-8725

"If you have a childhood memory, I can pretty much cocktail-whisper that into a drink," GERRY JOBE says. He grew up around the restaurant and bar industry, but when it came time to carve out his own career, he turned out to be the world's worst server. Luckily, the waiting game's loss was the cocktail drinker's gain. Born in Kelowna and raised in the Shuswap, Jobe learned the bar business from the ground up at Vancouver institutions like Fred's Uptown Tavern and BaBalu, where the house band was fronted by Michael Bublé. Jobe then helped open the Caprice Nightclub, a nocturnal Vancouver institution. Worn out and needing to get back to his roots and aging parents, Jobe returned to the Shuswap and eventually Kelowna. He connected with chef Rod Butters at RauDZ Regional Table and was given creative rein over the bar program as the restaurant's "liquid chef."

"Seeing that RauDZ was a farm-to-table restaurant, we thought that a standard bar program wouldn't work," he says. Jobe pushed beyond the fresh fruit martinis that were considered the cutting edge of local, and riffed on the restaurant's farm-to-plate philosophy by creating a farm-to-glass program. "Anything that hasn't been done before—that's my wheelhouse," says Jobe. He created housemade lavender and hon-eysuckle aromatics, concocted local beer reductions, and even made use of peach skins and peach flesh on his bar menu. The trouble he had was that when *he* got off shift, there were no bars serving interesting local handmade cocktails. "I knew that I had to incite a culture," he says, and he began reaching out to other local bartenders. This sparked the Okanagan cocktail movement in 2010.

Jobe currently freelances, consulting with restaurants in the valley on field-to-glass, which has become part of the culinary experience at any good restaurant in the Okanagan. Currently there are half a dozen energetic cocktail mixers who make their own infusions, botanicals,

PHOTO BY ADRIANPHOTOGRAPHERS.COM

Gerry Jobe

reductions, syrups, and tinctures and bring their creative personalities to bear wherever they are pouring in the valley. Find them, including Jobe, with the hashtag #okanagancocktailmovement on Twitter.

Stuart Klassen

STUART KLASSEN

SK Kitchen Consulting | 250-317-0010

"Thirty-two years later, and I'm still in love," STUART KLASSEN declares. He's talking about cooking professionally, and the man just oozes energy and passion for food. I met Klassen when he was executive chef of the Delta Grand Okanagan Resort and Conference Centre in Kelowna. Yes, he was in charge of a major kitchen with various outlets and banquet halls, but he always seemed to have time to do something special for a group, like making unforgettable popcorn snacks popped in guinea hen fat (it's like roast chicken and popcorn in the same mouthful).

After three decades as executive chef and director of food and beverage at hotels in Vancouver, Whistler, and Kelowna, he's now enjoying passing on his knowledge and experience to culinary arts students. As an instructor at Okanagan College, he works with chef apprentices going through the three-year program on their way to becoming journeyman Red Seal certified.

Klassen is also the past president of and now board chair for the Okanagan Chefs Association (OCA). "We've got a huge mentorship program with our junior chef members," he says. The OCA fundraises for and mentors junior members who compete nationally and even internationally. He's also been a chef instructor at the OCA's Growing Chefs initiative, in which professional chefs work with Grade 3 students over seven weeks to plant classroom gardens, harvest the produce, and then cook and eat what they've grown. "We change them for life!"

Klassen is now freelancing in the valley, consulting on new restaurant openeings such as Kettle Valley Plates in East Kelowna and the Black Bear Bar & Grill in downtown Kelowna.

JEFF KREKLAU

Routes Grill | 10058 Highway 97, Winfield, Lake Country | 250-766-0777 | routesgrill.com

A restaurant with a strip mall location on the highway and a menu that serves burgers, pastas, and pizzas might not jump out as a must-stop for locally grown and sourced foods and wines, yet that's what this place is. "Our salads, vegetables, and fruit all summer long come from Lake Country Culinary Farms, which is about two minutes up the road behind us," says JEFF KREKLAU, chef and co-owner of Routes Grill along with his wife, CODY, and their business partner, chef MICHAEL COATES. He notes that they also carry at least one selection from every Lake Country winery. "We really wanted to keep it as 'Lake Country' as possible, fresh from scratch, family-friendly, and casual." It's a perfect fit in this community, which Kreklau says is incredibly supportive; local hobby farmers and home gardeners often bring him huge bunches of basil, rhubarb, or other vegetables that they've grown in overabundance.

Kreklau was an executive chef in Edmonton when his and Cody's honeymoon trip through the Okanagan gave them an idea. Having spent many summer vacations in the Okanagan, both felt the pull to a slower pace of life and a food scene that really excited them with its potential. They moved to Kelowna, and Kreklau found work in the kitchen at Gray Monk Estate Winery. From there, he worked a season at Sparkling Hill and then settled in for a while at Cabana Bar and Grille, where he worked with chef Ned Bell and then became the catering chef for a year and a half.

When a small family-owned restaurant space in Winfield came up for sale, the Kreklaus and Coates, a friend and chef colleague from Edmonton, pooled their resources and opened Routes Grill in April 2012. From the start, they knew that their community needed a good family-friendly restaurant, but they saw the potential to make use of hyper-local ingredients. They also chose to focus on Lake Country wineries, and

Jeff Kreklau

luckily they have some stellar neighbours like Ex Nihilo, 50th Parallel, and Arrowleaf. Catering various Lake Country events also keeps the team at Routes Grill busy year-round. In 2015, they launched Ex Nihilo Vineyards' tasting room menu featuring pizzas and other offerings from a wood-fired pizza oven.

MARTIN LAPRISE

The Chef in Stead | West Kelowna | 250-878-8500 | thechefinstead.ca

MARTIN LAPRISE remembers his mother buying, and rationing, fresh cherries when he was a child growing up in Laval, Quebec. "They were imported from somewhere," he says. "Now I have a massive tree in my yard in West Kelowna that produces 160 pounds of cherries per year. I can't give them away. I always think of my mother and those cherries when I'm eating them right off the tree."

Laprise loved professional kitchens from the moment he was hired as a dishwasher at the age of 18. He attended culinary school in Quebec and three months after graduating opened his own fine dining restaurant. "I would not recommend that to any culinary student," he says. After three years he'd had enough, despite the success of the restaurant. He took his skills on the road, opening a mobile catering truck in Vancouver that served movie sets, and then to the seas, cooking on cruise ships. When his wife, KRISTIN PETURSON-LAPRISE, a sommelier, was offered a job at Mission Hill about a decade ago, the couple moved to the valley.

Laprise started his private-chef company, The Chef in Stead, in 2004 and has never looked back. His extrovert personality makes for always-fun events, whether it's a longtable farm-to-table dinner at Rabbit Hollow, essentially the couple's al fresco dining space behind their home in West Kelowna, or when Laprise takes his 1,400-kilogram (3,100-pound) barbecue trailer on the road to private catering events.

PHOTO BY DARREN HULL

Martin Laprise

Jason Leizert

JASON LEIZERT

Salted Brick | 243 Bernard Avenue, Kelowna | 778-484-3234 | saltedbrick.com

JASON LEIZERT has cooked his way around the world. He has cheffed in Australia, Hong Kong, Scotland, England, and Peru, to name a few countries. It was after a six-month stint in Peru that he felt like it was time to stop working for other people and open his own place. The Ontario native had friends in Kelowna and had been impressed by the Okanagan on previous visits. So in early 2014, Leizert opened Salted Brick, a narrow "charcuterie shop restaurant," as he calls it. "We make everything—except the cheeses—in-house." And he means everything. He orders and butchers whole animals for his homemade charcuterie, salami, and sausages. This also means that items like tongue, pâtés, and terrines are available, not for culinary showboating but as a way to use every bit of a carcass. Leizert also showcases locally grown and foraged products. On tap, he cycles between excellent local ciders, beers, and wines. At time of press, Leizert was opening Bread and Butter, an artisan bakery with a wood-burning oven and in-house flour mill, in Kelowna's downtown.

ROGER SLEIMAN

Quails' Gate Estate Winery | 3303 Boucherie Road, West Kelowna

250-769-2500 | quailsgate.com

When ROGER SLEIMAN came to work as the winery chef at Quails' Gate in 2006, local farmers were all trying to sell him specialty baby vegetables and fancy lettuces. It took Sleiman a while to convince some of them to plant basic staples of a restaurant kitchen, like potatoes, celery, carrots, fennel, and onions. Maybe because these items were not as glamorous, chefs in the region were having to go farther afield to source them. However, with a year-round restaurant like Old Vines at Quails' Gate Estate Winery—the 75-seat dining room expands to another 70 seats on the outdoor patio during the peak of the summer—Sleiman knew that it would be a win-win for both him and his growers, whether it was baby vegetables or onions. "The local farmers enjoy that security even before they plant," he says.

Sleiman, now culinary director and winery chef at Quails' Gate, still scours the valley for the best he can get. His favourite green bean grower, Irene, is nearing retirement age in Oyama, but until she stops, he'll make the effort to buy her excellent produce. "We deal with so many people, it's a struggle sometimes to keep up," he laughs.

Not only does Sleiman's menu showcase excellent local meats, Ocean Wise™ fish, vegetables, and fruits, but as a winery chef, he is constantly concerned with wine pairings when he's crafting dishes and writing menus. "I'm always balancing acidity," he explains, which is why his menus are tailor-made to accompany the cool-climate wines of the Okanagan and specifically from Quails' Gate—a complete taste of Okanagan terroir.

Roger Sleiman

CHRIS STEWART

Mission Hill Family Estate | 1730 Mission Hill Road, West Kelowna

250-768-6467 (Terrace Restaurant) | missionhillwinery.com

Growing up in Woodstock, New Brunswick, CHRIS STEWART had initial ambitions of being an architect. He was even accepted at the School of Architecture at McGill University in 1999, but he opted instead for a professional cooking program at Holland College's Culinary Institute of Canada in Charlottetown, PEI, when he realized he didn't want a career "sitting at a desk." "My dad didn't talk to me for about five months," he recalls. Nevertheless, Stewart pressed on with cooking, applying for work at the best restaurants no matter the pay or how unlikely his prospects. He was hugely influenced by the attention to detail and refined cuisine he saw in Thomas Keller's *The French Laundry Cookbook*. While interning at Toronto's Auberge du Pommier, Stewart applied and was accepted for other internships (known as *stages*, the French term for short-term kitchen internships that sometimes lead to permanent positions) at two Thomas Keller restaurants in the Napa Valley: the French Laundry and Bouchon Bistro. From there, Stewart worked his way up to the position of chef de cuisine, at only 27 years old, at the five-diamond restaurant, Eden, at the Rimrock Hotel in Banff.

"I then took a huge pay cut and took a two-position demotion," Stewart explains about his decision to "literally drop everything" when he was invited to join the kitchen team at the Fat Duck in Bray, Berkshire, UK. At the time, it was considered among the top three restaurants in the world. "We were in fifth gear the whole time," says Stewart of his two years there. "It taught us discipline, efficiency, and teamwork," lessons that Stewart now brings to his position as executive winery chef at Mission Hill Family Estate Winery.

Stewart is relishing the collaborative nature of his job with Mission Hill's larger team. "I meet with our winemakers all the time. They'll advise me of any changes that they're making with the wine portfolio, and we

PHOTO BY NAV SIDHU / MISSION HILL ESTATE WINERY

Chris Stewart

build our menus for the Terrace Restaurant and our private events off of the wine menu. It really drives how I create our plates." Stewart also is passionate about foraging in the gardens at Mission Hill. His team cultivates miner's lettuce, wood sorrel, chickweed, and other produce that grows in the impressive "varietal garden." Six grape varietals grow in proximity to other ingredients selected to pair with the various elements of the wine—a garden based around food and wine pairings. Stewart is also learning the art of beekeeping; he tends the six hives and then incorporates the honey into menus throughout the year. And, to add to the list, his kitchen does all its own charcuterie—"cellars are ideal environments for curing charcuterie"—and extreme amounts of canning.

Despite the swirl of activity and enthusiasm Stewart brings to Mission Hill, he's also keen on the fact that, as an avid skier in the winter, hard work and life are easier to balance in the Okanagan. Oh, and his father? "He came out from New Brunswick in April 2015 and played a round of golf here while there was still three feet of snow back home," Stewart laughs. His dad no longer worries about Stewart's pursuit of professional cooking over architecture.

Evelynn Takoff

EVELYNN TAKOFF

Micro Bar Bites | 1500 Water Street, Kelowna | 778-484-3500 | microkelowna.com

RauDZ Regional Table | 1560 Water Street, Kelowna | 250-868-8805 | raudz.com

A homegrown Kelowna farm girl involved in 4H, EVELYNN TAKOFF says food has always been an important part of her life. She first fell in love with the restaurant business as a server, especially the fast-paced environment and the adrenaline of a busy restaurant. After four years on the floor, she decided to broaden her skills and applied for a job in the kitchen. As it turned out, the back of the house had even more of the intensity, stress, and urgency that she loved. At 24 years old, she was hooked. She learned on the job, first at the Coast Capri Hotel in Kelowna under chef Monika Lauterbacher. Takoff then moved to Cabana Bar and Grille with chef Ned Bell and then over to RauDZ Regional Table in 2012. There she shared the position of restaurant chef with colleague Tyler Leeson, so on any given night, either one would be calling the shots in the open kitchen, visible to the packed house out front, and be in charge of the crew of one of the top restaurants in Kelowna. "It was terrifying, but I felt I was up to the challenge," Takoff says.

When Rod Butters and Audrey Surrao decided to expand their restaurant business to another space a few doors down from RauDZ, they installed Takoff as the chef de cuisine at Micro Bar Bites in 2013. It was a pivotal year for Takoff, as she was also selected to compete on *Top Chef Canada* and *Chopped Canada*. The episodes aired in 2014, catapulting her into the national arena of celebrity chefs at the age of 28. While the experiences were "really trying," they were also among the most challenging and rewarding of her career so far. "You just see how far you can stretch yourself physically, emotionally, and creatively," she says of these pressure-filled competitive cooking shows. Now back at work with the team at RauDZ and Micro Bar Bites, Takoff's "simple, fresh, local" cooking style is a perfect match for the focus of RauDZ's pioneering farm-to-table restaurant and Micro's hyper-local wine bar experience.

COURTESY OF TOURISM PENTICTON. PHOTO: ALLEN JONES

FARMERS' MARKETS

This information was correct at the time of press, but I've provided web addresses so you can check the hours and locations before you make plans to visit.

KELOWNA FARMERS' AND CRAFTERS' MARKET*

Corner of Springfield Road and Dilworth Drive

Wednesdays and Saturdays, early April to end of November, 8 AM to 1 PM

kelownafarmersandcraftersmarket.com

*Dogs not allowed at this market.

LAKE COUNTRY FARMERS' MARKET

10090 Bottom Wood Lake Road, Swalwell Park

Fridays, early June to late September, 3 PM to 7 PM

lakecountryfarmersmarket.webs.com

PEACHLAND FARMERS' AND CRAFTERS' MARKET

Heritage Park, Beach Avenue

Sundays, mid-May to late September, 10 AM to 2 PM

peachlandfarmersandcraftersmarket.ca

WESTBANK FARMERS' MARKET

2466 Main Street (West Kelowna)

Saturdays, late June to early September, 9 AM to 2 PM

westbankfarmersmarket.com

SOUTH OKANAGAN

OKANAGAN FALLS

OLIVER

OSOYOOS

PENTICTON

SUMMERLAND

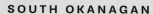

SOUTH OKANAGAN

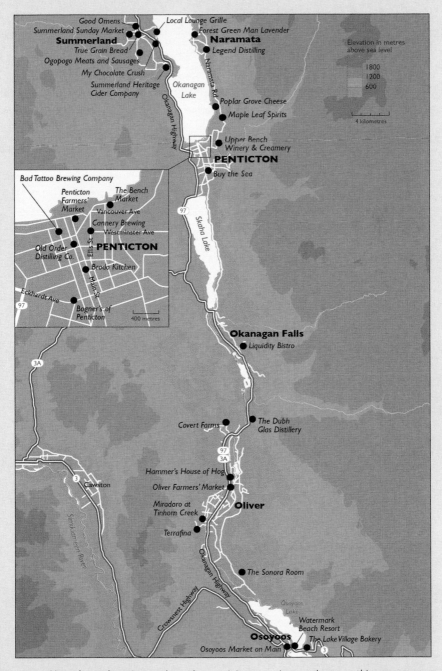

Good Omens
Local Lounge Grille
Summerland Sunday Market
Forest Green Man Lavender
Summerland
Naramata
True Grain Bread
Legend Distilling
Ogopogo Meats and Sausages
My Chocolate Crush
Okanagan
Lake
Summerland Heritage
Cider Company

Naramata Rd

Okanagan Highway

Poplar Grove Cheese
Maple Leaf Spirits

Upper Bench
Winery & Creamery
PENTICTON
Buy the Sea

Elevation in metres
above sea level

1800
1200
600

4 kilometres

Bad Tattoo Brewing Company

The Bench
Market
Penticton
Farmers'
Market
Vancouver Ave
Cannery Brewing
Westminster Ave
Ellis St
Old Order
Distilling Co.
PENTICTON
Broda Kitchen
Main St
Eckhardt Ave
97
Bogner's of
Penticton
400 metres

97
Skaha Lake

3A

Okanagan Falls
Liquidity Bistro

Covert Farms
The Dubh
Glas Distillery

97
3A

3
Cawston

Hammer's House of Hog
Oliver Farmers' Market
Miradoro at
Tinhorn Creek
Oliver
Terrafina

Similkameen River

Okanagan Highway

The Sonora Room

Crowsnest Highway

Osoyoos
Lake

Watermark
Beach Resort
The Lake Village Bakery
Osoyoos
Osoyoos Market on Main
3

Note that only artisans who welcome visitors on site are shown on this map.

SUMMERLAND IS ON THE WEST side of the lake, so it gets the first morning rays on its farms, vineyards, and beaches. It's the kind of community that you probably don't think exists anymore: cozy coffee shops, independent businesses, and a Main Street (free parking!) with one-storey storefronts. In the last few years, the number of organic farms, orchards, and vineyards in Summerland has been on the rise too.

Penticton sprawls between Okanagan Lake's south shore and Skaha Lake's north end. A channel connects the two lakes, and hundreds of locals and visitors alike can be found floating lazily on rafts and in inner-tubes from north to south on hot, cloudless days. It lies at the crossroads of the Naramata Bench, one of Canada's best wine routes (and now cheese, spirit, and cider routes too), and the wine and agricultural routes to the south.

Okanagan Falls is currently distinguishing itself with high-quality wineries and is home to some fantastic fruit stands and restaurants. Oliver and Osoyoos continue to be multicultural agricultural communities where Portuguese, Italian, Punjabi, and now Mexican and Latin American farming families grow incredible produce. Last but not least, there's the incredible success story of the sockeye salmon returning to Osoyoos Lake, thanks to the patient and determined work of the Okanagan Nation Alliance and First Nations activists and community members who didn't give up on restoring habitat and bringing salmon back to the interior, just as it had been for centuries before.

CERES SEED OILS

1458 Penticton Avenue, Penticton | 250-493-4869 | ceresoils.com

With vineyards all around us in the Okanagan, I wondered when an entrepreneur would start to make use of what I can only assume is a ridiculously abundant byproduct of winemaking. JUAN EDUARDO CACACE, an Argentina-born food scientist, spent decades working for the government and private sector in agricultural research and development. When in 2009 he decided it was time to work for himself, he launched Ceres Seed Oils.

The cold-pressed grapeseed oil is a revelation, with its luminescent green colour and fresh, nutty flavour. It's great for dipping, like a high-quality extra-virgin olive oil, or as a salad oil for homemade vinaigrettes. You could even cook or fry with it, but it would be a shame to cook the vibrant colours and flavour out of it. (It's different from grapeseed oil that you've likely had in the past, which has been processed at high temperatures to stabilize it and refined for clarity and for a long shelf-life, killing any nutritional value, fragrance, and flavours.) Cacace sources his grape seeds locally and doesn't add any colourants, preservatives, or additives. It's just freshly made oil produced in small batches. He also makes excellent cold-pressed pumpkin seed oil, pumpkin butter, and pumpkin meal (for smoothies) with Manitoba-grown pumpkin seeds, and cold-pressed sunflower seed oil from BC-grown sunflowers. Ceres Seed Oils uses only GMO-free ingredients. Find them at the Penticton Farmers' Market and at a few retailers in the Central Okanagan.

Juan Eduardo Cacace

Alex Sielmann

GORGEOUS GEORGIA'S

Penticton | 250-486-6189 | gorgeousgeorgias.com

"I'm finally giving in to the fact that I have a sweet tooth and limited self-control," laughs ALEX SIELMANN, owner of Gorgeous Georgia's, a Penticton-based handmade artisan ice cream and custom cakes enterprise. In the winter season, he is the pastry chef at Mica Lodge, a heli-skiing outfit near Revelstoke.

Sielmann began cooking professionally in 2005 and arrived in the Okanagan in 2007, working at Bogner's of Penticton and then, in 2011, at Joy Road Catering during the busy summer and fall season. From 2009 to 2011, he shuttled back and forth between Ontario and the Okanagan to attend Stratford Chefs School from October to May.

In 2015, Sielmann bought an existing handmade artisan ice cream outfit, Gorgeous Georgia's, that specialized in vegan and dairy-free creations, and he has taken it to a whole new level with his many years of professional cooking and acute sense of season and terroir learned in the Okanagan. He's kept the vegan and dairy-free options that launched Gorgeous Georgia's, like the local roasted hazelnut made with a coconut ice cream base, but he's added dairy-based ice creams to the lineup. "I use the best dairy that I can find and try to make a really beautiful product," he says. (His classic strawberry ice cream is sheer elegance—just ripe strawberries and delicious cream in a frozen bliss-inducing state.) A small production facility in an industrial area of Penticton is where Sielmann crafts his handmade ice creams, custom cakes, ice cream sandwiches, and such for various gourmet retailers in the valley. Find him in person at the Penticton Farmers' Market from April to October manning his reach-in ice cream cooler on a vintage tricycle.

NUMMERS! GOURMET

Summerland | 778-968-9459 | nummersgourmet.com

CAROLYNN PAWLUK was a graphic designer living in Buenos Aires when the 2008 recession put a real damper on "working remotely for well-paying North American clients." One evening, she passed by a pastry school in her barrio, and the sight of students in their chef's whites and hats reignited a childhood passion and got her thinking of a career change. She enrolled—the only English speaker in the group—and the instructors at the school rewarded her risk-taking.

She returned home to Vancouver and worked at Capers in the deli kitchen, then for two years as a baker-decorator at Whole Foods. She spent the next year and a half at the White Apron Pastry Co. (now closed) in Penticton making incredible pain au chocolate, croissants, and other fine pastry from scratch. Now she's created her own artisan food company, Nummers! Gourmet, where she makes the most of local ingredients to create pastries and confections like "wine gems" (gummies made with Okanagan wines), lollipops and fruit chews with local fruit, salted caramels, finely decorated sugar cookies, custom cakes, and other treats. Pawluk's handmade, whimsical treats are available at the Penticton Farmers' Market on Saturdays and the Summerland Sunday Market, through private orders, and through select retailers in the valley.

Carolynn Pawluk and sister, Leanne Pawluk

Peter Young

OKANAGAN WINELAND DRESSINGS

Naramata | wineland.ca

It's a very rare event for me to recommend that anyone buy bottled vinaigrette, simply because it's one of the easiest things to make—a glug from a good bottle of olive oil, a glug from a quality vinegar, some salt and pepper, and you've got it. That said, I cannot even come close to reproducing Okanagan Wineland's Roast Garlic Balsamic Vinaigrette, so I buy it, and I recommend that you do too. It's the dressing, after all, that launched a business.

PETER YOUNG was the chef at the Hillside Winery bistro along Naramata Road. So many customers asked to buy his housemade dressing that he realized he had a marketable product. In 2000, Peter and his wife, VALENCIA, launched Okanagan Wineland Dressings, and it's now their full-time gig. They added Raspberry & Black Pepper and Cilantro & Lime vinaigrettes to the lineup early on, and Fresh Herb & Garlic, Blackberry Basil, and Blueberry vinaigrettes more recently. All are made by hand in small batches with no added sugar. Now the bottles are sold all over the Okanagan in specialty food shops and at fruit stands and wineries, as well as throughout the BC Lower Mainland and on Vancouver Island.

Try the Roasted Garlic Balsamic on everything from tender new potatoes to roasted beets with goat cheese. I'm also a fan of the Cilantro & Lime on a perfectly ripe sliced avocado. Connect with Peter directly via email (pdsy@shaw.ca) to arrange a mail order.

THE LAKE VILLAGE BAKERY

6511 Main Street, Osoyoos | 250-495-3366 | thelakevillagebakery.ca

If you think your chances of finding macarons, or a Paris-Brest (a pra-line cream-filled choux pastry dessert), or a double-chocolate mousse bombe in Osoyoos are nil, it's understandable. But in fact, you'd be wrong. There just so happens to be a fantastic bread and pastry shop on Main where you can find those goodies—the Paris-Brest and macarons albeit are seasonal—and more.

The Lake Village Bakery was started and is run by SHANNON AND SEAN PELTIER, an ambitious young couple, both Red Seal chefs, who met during culinary arts training at Okanagan College in Kelowna. She worked at various establishments around Kelowna, including a stint at Okanagan Grocery Artisan Breads, learning from Monika Walker. He went on to apprentice with Rod Butters of RauDZ Regional Table for four years, then was drawn to the South Okanagan to work for chef Bernard Casavant while he was executive chef at Burrowing Owl's restaurant, the Sonora Room. Although Shannon and Sean loved the vibe of the South Okanagan, the seasonal nature of the restaurant scene didn't provide the stability they were after, so they put every cent they'd saved into opening their own business, a 1,000-square-foot bread and pastry shop.

Opened on June 1, 2012, the Lake Village Bakery has a very loyal local following. It's no surprise. The sourdough bread uses a wild yeast starter, organic local flours, and a three-day ferment to develop incredible flavours and textures. The Anarchist Loaf combines organic spelt, stone-ground whole wheat, white, and rye flours along with pumpkin, poppy, sunflower, and sesame seeds with ground flax. It's a signature loaf and definitely a local favourite. Restaurants like Miradoro at Tinhorn Creek, Nk'Mip Cellars, and the Watermark Beach Resort buy bread from the Lake Village Bakery. On the sweet side, the sourdough cinnamon buns and sourdough croissants, rich and

Stanley Zappa, Shannon Peltier, Peter Barcley

weighty things with a flaky golden crust, fly out the door. The bakery has been busy since it opened and now can operate year-round, just as the Peltiers hoped.

(As we were going to print, we received news that the Lake Village Bakery has partnered with Jo-Jo's Café, 8316 Main Street, Osoyoos, for all its baked goods retail seven days a week. The Lake Village Bakery will be open for bread-only purchases on Fridays and Saturdays.)

TRUE GRAIN BREAD

10108 Main Street, Summerland | 250-494-4244 | truegrain.ca

Many years ago, I made the pilgrimage to True Grain Bread, the artisan bread shop in Cowichan Bay on Vancouver Island where the movement for local, long-fermented, organic, no-additive, handmade breads seemingly was born in 2004. Nowadays I can mosey around to Summerland, because the second location of True Grain Bread has managed to settle on Main Street. "We get a lot of Islander tourists," and the sense of déjà vu is not coincidental, says TODD LAIDLAW, who co-owns True Grain Bread with partners Bruce and Leslie Stewart, who run the Vancouver Island location. The Summerland store, opened in 2012, was built to have the same "bread experience" as the original bakery, Laidlaw notes.

Part of the appeal is watching locally grown organic whole grain being stone-milled right in-store, before your eyes. "Nothing is added and nothing is taken away from the whole seed," says Laidlaw. You can also watch the bakers scaling the bread dough, smell loaves rising and baking, and then select from the assortment of European-inspired sweet and savoury baked items. Among others, there are wildly addictive ginger cookies, multigrain loaves, Red Fife sourdough, and a whole grain emmer loaf, which seems to be more popular in the grey winter months when Okanaganites are hunkering down. True Grain sells crazy amounts of a pastry called the Copenhagen, made with organic butter and ground almonds and hazelnuts. It's one the best-selling items at the bakery.

Laidlaw and the Stewarts chose Summerland as their second—and only—other location because, like Cowichan Bay, it is a small, tightly knit town "heavily rooted in agriculture," which is at the heart of True Grain Bread's reason for being. Their business is directly connected to local farms, from eggs to grains, and to organics; they needed to be in a community where those values resonated. Another compelling reason for locating in Summerland is the fact that the North Okanagan is a surprisingly productive grain-growing region, meaning they could source

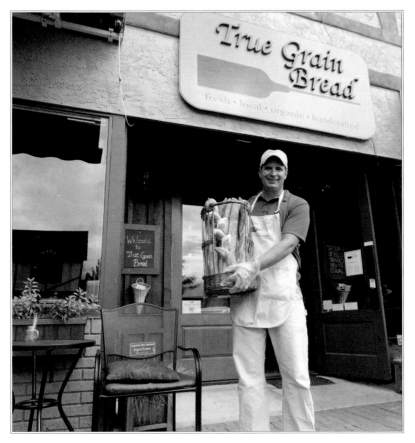

Todd Laidlaw

the local organic whole wheat, rye, spelt, emmer, and other ancient grains. (Fieldstone Organics is True Grain's main supplier; see page 45.)

True Grain also stocks a good selection of local cheeses, oils and vinegars, jams, honeys, and nut butters, plus the bakery's own line of pasta using the same true-to-the-grain, local, organic ancient varieties that go into the baked goods.

POPLAR GROVE CHEESE

1060 Poplar Grove Road, Penticton | 250-492-4575 | poplargrovecheese.ca

When my friends from Paris were visiting the Okanagan one summer, I sensed they were missing a few luxuries of home, like amazing cheese. Dashing off to Poplar Grove Cheese via Naramata Road, I bought rounds of Harvest Moon Washed Rind and Bench Blue, selecting ones that were well-aged, so much so that they barely held together in the mid-summer heat. I sliced a loaf of Joy Road sourdough and we had an afternoon *goûter* (snack). There were low, moaning sounds from them and not a lot of talk.

Cheesemaker extraordinaire GITTA PEDERSEN is a Dane who came to the Okanagan in the days when the valley was leaping forward in its number of wineries. She began to make cheese with a couple of recipes given to her by a cheesemaker in Australia. "I guess he didn't think I'd be much competition for him," she laughs. She learned by trial and error, making "seven Camemberts at a time" and aging them in the basement. Once the recipes and techniques for four cheeses were refined, Poplar Grove Cheese opened as a commercial cheesery in 2002.

"I'm not one for innovation. I'm a traditionalist," Pedersen says about the fact that Poplar Grove still makes only those four cheeses and the recipe has stayed "pretty much" the same from day one. Each cheese is made by hand in a rather laborious way that takes between four to six weeks, with each wheel being handled several times from the day of production, when it begins as milk from Dutchman Dairy in Sicamous, to the time it is heated, stirred, hand-moulded, and then aged and carefully checked, to when it is sold or arrives on your plate in a restaurant. Pedersen scales back production in the winter, and the cheese shop is open only on weekends in May, but daily from June through October.

The salty rind and mushroomy aromas of the Harvest Moon Washed make it my favourite of the four Poplar Grove cheeses, though really they are all excellent. The Bench Blue is creamy with a mottled blue salt-brined rind. The Tiger Blue is a hard, sharp blue-veined cheese.

Gitta Pedersen

And the Okanagan Double Cream Camembert is self-explanatory.

There's a bonus if you go to the cheese shop at Poplar Grove Road (not at Poplar Grove Winery—different entity altogether). It shares a tasting room with Lock & Worth Winery, a small-production, low-technology winery by Matthew Sherlock and Ross Hackworth. They follow the "natural wine" style of low-intervention, single-vineyard winemaking that allows the full expression of the grape, the time, and the place. Poplar Grove Cheese is also available at Naramata Store, the Bench Market, or other locations listed on Poplar Grove Cheese's website.

Shana Miller

UPPER BENCH WINERY & CREAMERY

170 Upper Bench Road South, Penticton | 250-770-1733 | upperbench.ca

SHANA MILLER was born in Nova Scotia, but she found both love (her husband, GAVIN) and a passion for making artisan cheese in the Okanagan. Shana worked her way up at Poplar Grove Cheese, becoming head cheesemaker until 2006. In May 2012, Gavin and Shana opened the doors to their own enterprise, Upper Bench Winery & Creamery, a lovely tasting room and cheesemaking facility right on Naramata Road; Gavin's vineyard rises up the slope behind the shop. Shana makes award-winning cheeses on-site using pasteurized cow's milk from Dutchmen Dairy in Sicamous. Her seven excellent cheeses come in a wide range of styles: from the signature Okanagan Gold, a washed-rind, semi-soft, buttery-smooth cheese that demands to be paired with a good baguette, to the pleasing tang of the blue-veined King Cole. You can order cheese plates and Upper Bench wines by the glass, sit on the patio, and watch the world—or at least the winery tourists—go by on Naramata Road.

MY CHOCOLATE CRUSH

168 Jewell Place, Summerland (by appointment only)

250-462-1576 | mychocolatecrush.com

LESLEY VAISANEN says that opening her chocolate business in July 2014 came about when she asked herself: "If you could do anything, what would you do?" This mother of five had always loved the visual artistry of chocolates, so she threw herself into becoming a chocolatier as her kids grew up and became more independent. She took a number of courses at the Ecole Chocolat in Vancouver and the Callebaut Chocolate Academy in Chicago, then went to Maui to intern with a chocolatier.

Vaisanen's shop is in the lower level of her home, which was custom-built to accommodate the business. She goes to great length to source quality and ethical chocolate, and she agonizes over packaging. She makes each chocolate herself, unless things get very busy and she has to call in a helper.

The method Vaisanen uses to make her line of chocolates is time-consuming and labour-intensive. "It's a three-day process from start to finish," she says. She rotates through a portfolio of 52 different chocolates seasonally, carrying about 30 different chocolates at any given time. "I'm a little type A," she laughs. But the work is paying off as the buzz builds for her inventive and quality creations. I particularly like the Summer Orchard Collection that Vaisanen crafts out of local berries and orchard fruit, but she also puts together irresistible combos like pecan and bourbon with a hint of chili spice.

Vaisanen also commutes (really!) between Summerland and Nassau, Bahamas, where she is the head chocolatier at the prestigious Graycliff, a luxury hotel resort with a restaurant, its own in-house cigar company, and a bean-to-bar chocolate division. The opportunity came out of the blue, but Vaisanen feels she's won some sort of lottery, with a busy summer creating chocolates for winery and corporate clients and customers in the Okanagan and winters making chocolates in the Bahamas.

Lesley Vaisanen

Richard Haverkamp

BACKYARD BEANS

3116 Johnson Road, Summerland | 250-494-5279 | backyardbeanscoffee.com

RICHARD HAVERKAMP says that when he owned his Volkswagen repair shop, no one *really* ever wanted to have to see him. He started roasting coffee in his garden shed at home in Trout Creek, Summerland, on a hunch that he could get out of the car repair business and into something where every customer was *very* happy to see him. That was 2003, and by 2006, Backyard Beans was a home-based, full-time job for him and his wife, LIZ LE MARE.

They seem to have a fairly ideal set-up. A newly built barn in their backyard (hence the name) houses their 36-year-old Probat bean roaster, which handles only 12 kilograms (26 pounds) of beans at a time—yet they still manage to roast a tonne of beans per month, on average. They source premium grade, sustainably grown beans in small lots. Haverkamp and Le Mare are proud of their beans, trying their best to source from quality farms that are fair-trade, UTZ-certified, certified organic, and operated in accordance with the Rainforest Alliance. Haverkamp notes that they use three beans that aren't certified organic (from Cuba, Brazil, and Burundi) but "are organic by default"; it's just that the growers don't have the funds for organic audits. Backyard Beans' coffee bags are even compostable (stickers removed). Each bag is filled and labelled by hand.

It is telling that premium coffee shops like the Bench Market and Good Omens buy from Backyard. And there's always a lineup at the Penticton Farmers' Market, where every customer is happy to see Haverkamp. Just as he'd hoped.

LONE TREE COFFEE

9503 Cedar Avenue, Summerland | 250-494-0064 | lonetreecoffee.com

When ROCHELLE AND DARIN FAIR moved from the West Coast to Summerland in 1996, it was a make-your-own-employment scenario in their new community. They decided to bring the then-budding coffee culture to Summerland, opening the Beanery Coffee Company that same year. Intially, being new to the coffee industry, they bought beans from a Vancouver roaster while they worked to establish an independent coffee house that served the community's needs. In 2000, they bought a refurbished roaster, enabling them to roast beans themselves for a fresher result and to further their experience with coffee. There was a lot of trial and error; batches of under-roasted beans and burnt batches had to be thrown out. Darin, however, persevered and eventually became adept at achieving ideal roasts, often working outside of café hours to give the process the attention it deserved. The demands of a café business plus their growing family of four kids were mounting, so when an offer to buy the business came in, it was a bittersweet decision to sell.

The Fairs sold Beanery Coffee Company in 2008 to Pete and Aline Borsboom, who had just moved their family to Canada. The Fairs kept the roaster, and from a new location, continued to supply the Beanery and other cafés and grocery stores with fresh roasts. They also helped the Borsbooms, who brought baking experience with them from Holland, transition to café life.

In 2013, the Fairs rebranded as Lone Tree Coffee to avoid confusion between the Beanery café and their roastery. Their new Diedrich roaster uses infrared heat—a substantial energy saver, especially coupled with the oxider (an after-burner), which eliminates air pollution from the roasting process and further reduces energy consumption by 50 percent. It also gives Darin a whole new level of roasting precision.

Lone Tree has a lineup of eight different coffees, including a decaf.

Rochelle Fair

They only roast to order. Lone Tree still supplies the Beanery and other local grocery, wholesale, and individual clients, but now has a growing online store as well, with shipments being sent as far away as New York City. However, when Rochelle drops off an order in person to a customer, which she loves to do, it means the beans are just out of the roaster. In Rochelle's "perfect world," Lone Tree's inventory shelves are bare on a Friday and they start roasting the next week's coffee again on Monday.

Heather and Stewart Glynes

THE BENCH MARKET

368 Vancouver Avenue, Penticton | 250-492-2222 | thebenchmarket.com

STEWART AND HEATHER GLYNES decided in 2009 to leave the Lower Mainland and raise their then one-year-old in the Okanagan. Stewart accepted the role of head chef at the Bench Market, a bustling café and fine foods market in Penticton where Vancouver Avenue rises up to meet the Naramata Bench. Four years later, Stewart and Heather took the reins as owners. They added two more children to their household, and their family photo hangs in the Bench right about where the morning lineup begins for a Backyard Beans latte, the weekend fave of a Bench Benny, or homemade doughnuts on Fridays.

One of the main draws for Stewart, who worked as a chef in Vancouver, was that he was closer to more outstanding growers, incredible fresh ingredients, and top-quality products than he had ever been in the city. Heather took to the retail side of the business—"our focus is on supporting both new and established artisans in the region," she says—and has a lot of pride in the well-chosen local products on the shelves. They go on road trips to source quality regional ingredients, so the Bench is a one-stop shop for anyone looking for the top products of the Okanagan. They also range farther afield for good olive oils and spices, because good cooks need those things too.

Groups of cyclists recharge in the sun on the patio during their rides along Naramata Road with the Bench's famous granola and yogurt, and locals dash in to buy cheese, a Bench-made take-and-bake pizza, or one of the deli salads. A visit to the Bench is a quintessentially local experience, from the menu to the products to the people.

GOOD OMENS

13616 Kelly Avenue, Summerland | 250-494-3200 | goodomens.ca

JASON EMBREE, a Red Seal chef, spent time in restaurant kitchens in the Okanagan and Shuswap before starting Good Omens, a coffee house in a renovated bungalow set in a residential neighbourhood just a few blocks off Summerland's Main Street. Of course coffee is a mainstay here, with Summerland's Backyard Beans organic brews and espresso. The sandwiches are made with excellent local bread, and the house-smoked and house-brined meats are also local, free-range, and medication-free. The soups are made from scratch, and specialties like the kale, beet, and apple salad smack of the Okanagan. Good Omens also serves a surprising selection of local wines and beers, and the cask nights featuring local breweries are proving extremely popular, as are the live music nights in Good Omen's large backyard during the summer.

Jason Embree

Sam Tibbitt

HAMMER'S HOUSE OF HOG

6607 Station Street (Lion's Park), Oliver | 250-535-3700

Hammer's is a cash-only BBQ shack in Lion's Park in Oliver. It might be the valley's best-kept secret, and it's a regular road trip for my husband and me. SAM TIBBITT makes authentic Southern slow-smoked pulled pork with a choice of South Carolina Mustard, North Carolina Red, Kansas City Sweet & Spicy, or Alabama Great White sauce on a bun, in a wrap, or just naked in a to-go cup. He puts a spoonful of coleslaw on top and we're in hog heaven. There's beef brisket on Thursdays. In keeping with strict BBQ convention, no diet drinks are available. The shack stays open until Tibbitt runs out of pork that day. It's also a one-man show, so check Hammer's House of Hog's Facebook page for the odd day or weekend that Tibbitt chooses to take off.

LOCAL LOUNGE GRILLE

12817 Lakeshore Drive South, Summerland | 250-494-8855 | thelocalgroup.ca

The idea of the best BC wines and craft beers by the glass—or beer flight—paired with menus built upon seasonal Okanagan and West Coast ingredients at their peak of flavour just seems so obvious now. But in 2009, it was still daring to be so committed to a local culinary vibe that you'd wrap your entire restaurant's name around it. That's what CHRISTA-LEE MCWATTERS BOND AND CAMERON BOND did, however, when they opened Local Lounge Grille in Summerland in 2009, and it's been a place to gather for locavores ever since.

McWatters Bond—daughter of Harry McWatters, founder of Sumac Ridge Estate Winery, BC's first estate winery in the 1980s—grew up in one of Canada's winemaking first families. She met her now husband and business partner, Bond, as a wine representative for Sumac Ridge, when he was managing the Hume Hotel in Nelson, BC. Since opening Local Lounge, they've had an excellent track record of showcasing great talent, notably chefs Paul Cecconi (see page 230), followed by Lee Humphries (see page 235), and now BRADLEY CLEASE as executive chef, whom I first met when he opened his outstanding Summerland restaurant, Vanilla Pod, in the mid-2000s. Go to Local Lounge Grille for the food and wine, but linger over the waterfront views from the patio, because on a summer day, it's a quintessential slice of Okanagan.

Christa-Lee McWatters Bond and Cameron Bond

Samantha and Mike Stokes

BUY THE SEA

2100 Main Street, Penticton | 250-492-3474

2231 Louie Drive, Governors Market, West Kelowna | 250-768-3474 | buythesea.ca

Growing up in Alberta, I did not have a lot of ocean fish in my diet. But that certainly is the case in the Okanagan, with the local sockeye run that comes all the way up the Columbia from the Pacific and into Oysoyoos Lake, plus the well-established connections with West Coast fishing and seafood-gathering communities. Living in the Okanagan, I have become very picky not just about what fish and seafood I buy, but about how it is acquired by the fishers and the fishmonger. I'm aware that every single fish purchase matters in the battle against overfishing, bycatch issues, and ethical and fair economics for those who try to make a living by sustainably harvesting what is now an endangered traditional wild industry.

Buy the Sea became a member of Vancouver Aquarium's Ocean Wise™ program in 2012, and owners MIKE AND SAMANTHA STOKES promote sustainable seafood and fish choices to their customers. I'm a keen fan of the in-store café's halibut and chips. It's a generous piece of fresh, lightly battered Pacific halibut that is cooked at the perfect temperature in clean oil, and as an Alberta-born transplant, I feel like I've discovered buried treasure every time.

Aside from lovely mussels, fresh oysters, and fish, Buy the Sea carries excellent local companion products on its retail shelves, such as Little Miss Chief smoked sockeye and Okanagan Wineland Dressings. In fact, Okanagan Wineland's Cilantro & Lime Vinaigrette is Mike's go-to quick marinade tip for fresh Pacific halibut. The store might also have the happiest staff going! I'm greeted by name every time, and we chat about our respective comings and goings. I know that this has little to do with food, but it does have a lot to do with community.

ROAD 17 ARCTIC CHAR

303 Road 17, Oliver (no on-site sales) | 250-485-7408 | road17char.ca

This might be the most unlikely story in this book. In 2010, GARY KLASSEN and family moved to the South Okanagan because they loved the area. They also wanted to start a business they could operate as a family. The original plan was to start a specialty year-round greenhouse operation that would sell to chefs and restaurants. They bought flat land and an orchard about halfway between Oliver and Osoyoos. They drilled a well on their property and found that they had abundant access to clean, cold water that stayed at 12 degrees Celsius year-round. "As soon as we discovered that we had water at 12 degrees Celsius, I pursued the idea of arctic char," says Klassen. "I thought of raising fish."

It may seem like a leap, but Klassen had been looking around at all possibilities. He remembered a conversation in which a friend had suggested that he look at businesses that were difficult to get into. "He said, 'The stuff that's easy has all been done,'" remembers Klassen. Well, it wasn't easy to open the first inland aquaculture outfit in the Okanagan—permitting took two years. And very strict regulations for the 8,000-square-foot facility, aquaculture tanks, waste removal, and water quality at the end of the process needed to be addressed. "The farm was built around that challenge," says Klassen.

In December 2012, the Department of Fisheries and Oceans granted Klassen a licence to hatch and raise his first batch of artic char. (It would take 18 months to two years to grow fish to market weight.) Now Road 17 Arctic Char Okanagan-raised arctic char are in Codfathers Seafood Market, in Buy the Sea, and on restaurant menus at Burrowing Owl, Liquidity Bistro, Miradoro, and elsewhere in the valley. It's an Ocean Wise™-approved choice and has a SeaChoice rating as "best choice." The fish are raised without hormones, antibiotics, or medications in cold, clean, pathogen-free water from the farm's well. Klassen knows he's up against the (justifiably) negative image of fish farming, but he has the

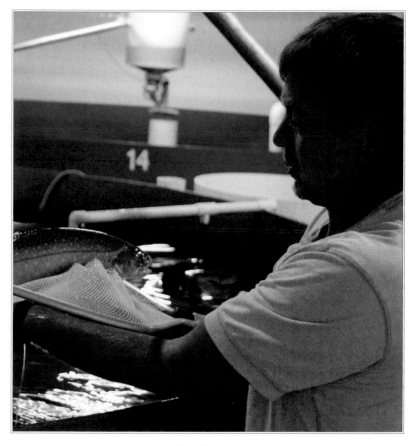

Gary Klassen

support of some of Canada's top seafood-savvy chefs like Robert Clark, Ned Bell, Jeff Van Geest, and Lee Humphries. Klassen knows that he might have to win over some customers, but an environmentally sound, family-operated fish-raising facility in the South Okanagan certainly has people talking. "It wakes people up to the fact that it can be done inland."

OKANAGAN NATION ALLIANCE

syilx.org

Stories abound in First Nations communities of the epic sockeye salmon runs that used to occur each fall in the small creeks and streams of the Okanagan lakes chain in southwestern interior BC. It was an especially important food, trading, and cultural event for Syilx-speaking First Nations who flowed between the Okanagan territories south and north of the US border as far up as the Nicola Valley. But that was three to four generations ago. Nine hydroelectric dams were built along the Columbia River, and 1,000 kilometres (620 miles) of natural waterways in the Columbia-Okanagan river systems were altered and straightened, causing serious disruption to the migratory routes of the ocean-going sockeye.

"There was a whole generation that didn't have a chance to fish," Osoyoos First Nations band member and fisher JOHN HALL tells me one still August day on the shores of Osoyoos Lake. Tears well up in his pale green eyes as he talks about the scary drop in sockeye stocks in the valley just in his lifetime. It wasn't just the loss of a food he was mourning; the *n'titxw* (salmon) is one of the Four Food Chiefs, or foundational cultural foods of the Syilx people.

By the mid-1990s, sockeye stocks in Osoyoos, Skaha, and Okanagan Lakes had reached a critical low. Fewer than 5,000 sockeye were returning to the Canadian lakes, only half of which were female sockeye carrying eggs. Like the sockeye that used to return and spawn in the nearby Similkameen River system, the Okanagan sockeye were almost lost. Almost.

In 2003, a small pilot project began to reintroduce sockeye salmon to Skaha Lake (south of Okanagan Lake but north of Osoyoos Lake)—the result of years of transborder negotiations and trust-building between waterway authorities in the US and Canada. Spearheaded by the Okanagan Nation Alliance—seven First Nations communities in Canada and the Confederated Tribes of the Colville Reservation in the US, all Syilx-speaking peoples—it has proven, so far, to be a long, slow, but steady success story.

Thanks to a combination of habitat restoration initiatives, hatchery and

PHOTO BY INGRID JARRETT

John Hall

Pauline Terbasket,
Executive Director of ONA

fish passage science, and coordinated stewardship between the Okanagan Nation Alliance and the Department of Fisheries and Oceans, the sockeye have been returning in numbers that have surprised even the most optimistic supporters. The sockeye returned in droves to Osoyoos Lake in 2010, and recreational fishing was allowed. In 2011, the Okanagan Nation Alliance began a fishery operation on Osoyoos Lake, catching salmon in August and distributing food to communities, but also selling to fish shops and restaurants in the Okanagan Valley and Lower Mainland. The good-sized return—some 450,000—to Osoyoos Lake in 2012 allowed the commercial fishery to operate for the full month of August. Thanks to the Okanagan Nation Alliance and key people at the Department of Fisheries and Oceans, like Richard Bussanich and Howie Wright, sockeye has returned to First Nations homes and feasts and to restaurant menus in Okanagan wine country.

Okanagan sockeye is certified Ocean Wise™, and restaurants and chefs in the valley love the new source of local, sustainable fish. Buy Okanagan Nation Alliance sockeye at Codfathers Seafood Market in Kelowna or find it in restaurants in the valley during the sockeye run in late July and August.

GARNET HOLLOW ORGANIC FARM & LOCALMOTIVE ORGANIC DELIVERY

27218 Garnett Valley Road, Summerland | 250-488-7615 (Garnet Hollow Organic Farm)

250-462-7604 (LocalMotive) | localmotive.ca

THOMAS TUMBACH arrived in Summerland as a five-year-old. His parents had retired from farming a 100-acre grain farm in Saskatchewan and bought a piece of residential land in Trout Creek, where they grew a plentiful home garden. "I don't recall being keenly interested," Tumbach says about helping out. "I just sort of took for granted that there was all this homegrown food around." He *was* interested in science, though, so when the time came, he enrolled at the University of British Columbia (UBC). He considered both forestry and agriculture for his major, but agriculture won out. One of Tumbach's professors, an exiled Chilean agriculturalist, opened his eyes to the social value of agriculture, and something clicked. He graduated with a bachelor's degree in agriculture and sustainable land and food systems. "I left university with an understanding of how food affects the social health of a community, the benefits of social opportunities and connectedness, especially how it affects our lives every day."

Thomas met Celina Deuling (now CELINA TUMBACH), a forestry conservation student, in classes that overlapped at UBC. Deuling grew up on a farm in Lumby, where her family raised pigs before her dad switched to forestry as the pork industry crashed. Thomas and Celina married and moved back to the Okanagan to start a life together. "We wanted to start our own business in line with our ethical beliefs of food and society," says Tumbach.

In 2005, they started LocalMotive, a Community Supported Agriculture (CSA) home delivery service that sourced high-quality organic foods from a dozen farmers in the South Okanagan and delivered weekly to homes as far north as Summerland. The Tumbachs leased farmland in 2011 and put LocalMotive's CSA on hold for three years while they

Thomas Tumbach with one of his farmer-suppliers for LocalMotive, Andrew Atherton, photographed with Atherton's sons Dominic and Benjamin

climbed the steep learning curve of small-scale organic farming and raised their growing family of four youngsters. By 2014, LocalMotive was revived. In 2015, the Tumbachs bought farmland in Summerland and started their own Garnet Hollow Organic Farm. (Find them online at localmotive.ca.)

The Tumbachs also co-founded (along with Jennifer Vincent) an ingenious winter project called the Farm Bag Fundraiser program. Schools or other groups gather CSA subscribers, and a portion of the CSA sales go back to that group. Boxes of food are delivered to a drop-off location, like a school, and subscribers fill a bag of whatever food they want for that week. In the first few years, the Farm Bag Fundraiser has put $50,000 into local community groups' bank accounts while giving local farmers a reliable cash flow in the winter months.

Arlene and Dave Sloan

MATHESON CREEK FARM

29 Eastside Road, Okanagan Falls | 250-497-8989 | mathesoncreekfarm.ca

When we moved to the Okanagan, I found it quirky that locals would travel to a fruit stand several kilometres away instead of shopping at one closer to home. To the untrained eye (or nose or palate), every fruit stand seemed to be selling the same array of fruits or vegetables. But early on, my sister-in-law insisted that we drive to Okanagan Falls one day to buy peaches from Matheson Creek Farm, and I've been going back there ever since. I have found other peach sources closer to home that I am fond of, but I still frequent Matheson Creek Farm for grapes, peaches, apples, corn, and a few other items.

DAVE AND ARLENE SLOAN's Matheson Creek Farm overlooks Skaha Lake along Eastside Road. It's open August through October and carries 20 varieties of apples, eight types of peaches, four types of pears, several strains of plums and prune plumes, and various field crops like peaches and cream corn, onions, garlic, squash, and pumpkins. The Sloans take the utmost care with their food, picking in the cool of the early morning and making sure the fruits and produce go directly into their on-farm cooler or into the straw-bale farm market to be sold right away. "We have full control over every piece of fruit or vegetable that we sell," says Arlene. Matheson Creek Farm is also a fixture at the Penticton Farmers' Market on Saturdays as soon as their early August-ripening Sunrise apples are ready. In 2014, the Sloans took five apple varieties from their farm to the Royal Agricultural Winter Fair in Toronto. All entries did very well, but their Pinova apple—a cross between a Golden Delicious, a Cox's Orange Pippin, and a Duchess of Oldenburg—won first place in its categories.

FOREST GREEN MAN LAVENDER

620 Boothe Road, Naramata | 250-488-8365 | forestgreenman.com

I hesitate to divulge my secret source for Balaton sour cherries, but even my husband and I can eat only so many of these blood-red beauties each year. We pit and freeze kilos of them every July for pies and smoothies, and they are the cherries for my "famous" sour cherry-apricot jam that I'm sure I could sell for $150 a jar *if* I ever let go of some of my stash—which will never happen. The Balatons come from Forest Green Man Lavender, the most beautiful farm you'll ever see, with its signature lavender fields rolling down the hillsides toward the lake right in the village of Naramata.

Odetta Mathias, a widowed mother of three, moved to Penticton in 1955 after being the first woman to earn a master's degree in agriculture and soils at the University of British Columbia. She remarried, becoming Odetta Keating, and together with her second husband, Ken Keating, bought a picturesque piece of farmland in Naramata in 1962. She kept a large garden on the farm along with the fruit trees and taught chemistry at Penticton High School. When she retired from teaching, she sold the farm to her son, DOUG MATHIAS, and travelled to Tanzania to volunteer with Cuso International, a non-profit development organization. She returned to Penticton after her travels and continued to volunteer in the community until her death in 2002.

DOUG AND KAROLINA BORN-TSCHÜEMPERLIN now run the farm as Forest Green Man, with its fruit trees, 2,500 lavender plants, small vegetable market garden, farm store, art gallery, and two seasonal rental cottages. Besides Balatons, they grow the lighter-coloured Montmorency sour cherries; Bartlett, Anjou, and Bosc pears; peaches; Italian prune plums; and Ambrosia and Gala apples in their orchard. "In order to make a living now, you have to diversify," says Born-Tschüemperlin of the dizzying array of products she makes and sells on the farm to the events they host. "You have to have something going on every week!"

Mathias's distilled essential lavender oils are sold in the shop along

Karolina Born-Tschüemperlin and Doug Mathias

with culinary and perfume lavenders and various other fine lavender products such as honey, vinegar, sugar, and tea. I'm partial to Born-Tschüemperlin's herbes de Provence blend as well as the simple but excellent lavender pepper. Even though I have my own lavender plants (bought at Forest Green Man), I still can't replicate her blends. Recently, she has been developing bitters for Legend Distilling's tasting room in Naramata, using her lavender and herbs and some foraged wild products, such as orange sumac and rosehips. The market garden has seasonal produce, from garlic and onions to heirloom tomatoes. Sometimes I stop by simply to drink in the vista of the lavender fields, the perfect rows of 17 varieties that bloom in succession and buzz with local honeybees. The farm's shop and the new art gallery are open from the beginning of May until after the fall harvest.

WHAT THE FUNGUS

Summerland | 250-809-9217 | wtfmushrooms.ca

Fresh mushrooms are big business in Canada, especially in BC. According to Agriculture and Agri-Food Canada, our country is one of the world's largest exporters of fresh mushrooms in the world, shipping over $110 million each year, largely to the US. And BC is by far the largest commercial mushroom producer of all provinces. Most mushroom farms are large-production, high-volume outfits that produce the button, portobello, and crimini mushrooms that are readily available in grocery stores. Those are not the sort of mushrooms that end up in a book about food artisans.

In 2011, BRIAN CALLOW, then 29 years old, had a degree in hotel tourism management and had worked in fine dining restaurants across Canada. Looking to start his own business, he came upon the idea of fresh, locally grown gourmet mushrooms. "It was like I had discovered a secret that only a few people knew about, and I wanted to learn everything," he recalls. However, when he looked for educational opportunities to learn about small-scale artisan and exotic mushroom cultivation in Canada, he found none. Instead, he cobbled together his own education, turning to the Internet, reading as many books on mushroom cultivation as he could find, and finally attending workshops with Paul Stamets on Cortes Island, BC, and then with Ja Schindler in Eugene, Oregon. This, and a partnership with arborist THOR CLAUSEN, finally launched Callow's business.

Currently, What The Fungus is the only mushroom farm in the Okanagan. Callow grows mushrooms outdoors in unheated greenhouses, using local recycled wood waste as a medium (as opposed to the pasteurized manure-based beds in heated barns that commercial mushrooms are grown in year-round). Not only does this save a lot of energy, but it forces Callow to grow mushroom strains that work in the seasonal temperatures and by controlling the humidity in the greenhouses from April to November, like Blue Oyster, King Oyster, and Lion's Mane to name

Brian Callow

a few. He's constantly adding new mushrooms—he currently has 70 edible strains in his collection—and he's even experimenting with producing local mushrooms like Tree Oyster, Aspen Oyster, and Shaggy Mane. Most fresh mushrooms are delicate and have a very short shelf life after being picked, so Callow harvests and delivers on the same day to restaurants—and picks just before selling at the Penticton Farmers' Market.

Callow also sees opportunity in filling the educational gap. His 30-day internships have proven popular, with interns coming from all over North America to exchange free labour for education.

Natalie and Thomas Fischer with daughters

OGOPOGO MEATS & SAUSAGES

9504 Alder Street, Summerland | 778-516-5595 | ogopogomeats.com

Ogopogo Meats & Sausages is not a business you'll stumble across accidentally; you really have to go looking for it. It's up a few winding switchbacks in an industrial part of Summerland. That said, it's worth the effort for the selection of free-range, grass-fed, grass-finished (grain-free), and antibiotic-free lamb, venison, beef, and bison. Yes, you have to cook grass-fed red meats like beef and bison with a bit more care and attention than a marbled striploin from a big-box store, but I prefer the flavour and the nutritional boost of their iron-rich composition. Ogopogo Meats is also where I go for whole (frozen) duck and (fresh or frozen) chicken, antibiotic-free pork, and sausages that are MSG-free, lactose-free, and gluten-free and have no added nitrites.

THOMAS FISCHER, the butcher and owner, is always up for an in-depth conversation about his products. He received a master's degree in food science in Germany, a multi-year course of study and the country's highest qualification in meat science. He's even a little bit arrogant—he'll tell you this himself—but it's because he has complete control and confidence in his product. If you don't want to go adventuring in the hills of Summerland to find Ogopogo, you'll find its products at a number of specialty food stores in the valley.

TONY'S MEATS LTD.

1848 Main Street, Apple Plaza, Penticton | 250-492-5578 | tonysmeats.ca

TONY CRAVEIRO came to the South Okanagan in 1984, newly wed to his Portuguese-Canadian wife. Despite having worked with his father in the family meat-cutting business in the Azores Islands, Portugal—from the tender age of 11—he couldn't find work in Canada as a butcher. Instead, he spent 12 years working in the orchards in the valley. "I loved it," he says in his amiable accent. When he realized he could make a go of his own meat business in Penticton, Craveiro opened Tony's Meats in 1998, a custom butcher shop and specialty grocery. You can't miss him when you walk into the shop. His booming voice carries as he banters with his loyal customers about the ideal thickness of a pork chop or the secrets of his signature Maui ribs. He custom cuts fresh meat to order, and has as excellent line of his own house-made sausages, burgers, and smoked and cured meats like bacon and ham. The shop is also chock full of excellent Okanagan-made honey, sauces, marinades, and dips.

Chris Martens, Amanda Arlitt, Nicole Armstrong, and Tony Craveiro

Ron and Patt Dyck

CANNERY BREWING COMPANY

198 Ellis Street, Penticton | 250-493-2723 | cannerybrewing.com

When my husband and I came out to the Okanagan a decade ago, we ended a day of house hunting at the pub down in Naramata. My first swig of the smooth, malty Naramata Nut Brown Ale sealed the deal. When I told this story recently to PATT DYCK, who owns and runs Cannery Brewing Company with her husband, RON DYCK, she smiled. She told me that I'm not the only one with such a story. I imagine it's a heavy responsibility that your beer can change lives.

I'm trying to think back to the year 2000 and whether I even knew the term *craft beer*. That's when the Dycks sold their beloved Country Squire Restaurant in Naramata, after a run of 23 years, to launch a small brewery, which they hoped would afford them a saner schedule. One of their Country Squire chefs was a keen home brewer, and they picked up the idea from him. "We were lonely missionaries," says Patt of those early days. But "one beer at a time," they built a loyal following for their unpasteurized, unfiltered craft beers that don't shy away from big flavours.

Cannery Brewing makes Naramata Nut Brown, Paddles Up Pale Ale, Lakeboat Lager, IPA, Squire Scotch Ale, and Blackberry Porter year-round. They also make a half-dozen seasonal beers in the summer and one-off artisan creations and cask-conditioned beers. In 2015, Cannery Brewing moved to a custom-built new facility in downtown Penticton to expand production and to have a more accessible tasting lounge a couple of blocks off the beach, where you can stop in for a "bite and a flight." The taproom menu features local Penticton products. Cannery Brewing also contracts with Farmersdotter to make a Naramata Nut Brown Ale Honey Mustard, which happens to go quite nicely with a quality sausage and a pint of Cannery beer.

THE DUBH GLAS DISTILLERY

8486 Gallagher Lake Frontage Road, Oliver | 778-439-3580 | thedubhglasdistillery.com

GRANT STEVELY had big dreams and a small budget. After 18 years at Sunshine Village Ski & Snowboard Resort in Banff, Alberta, he was looking to build a business of his own. As a self-described "appreciator of single malt whisky," and noticing the growth in the single malt market worldwide, he began to seriously consider opening his own distillery. "We have the raw materials in Canada," he adds. This was 2010, and the liquor laws in BC still disadvantaged small craft distillers. Nevertheless, the Okanagan seemed a good bet, given that he could buy land and build in the south and would be surrounded by a wine industry that already attracted attention, culinary tourism, and culinary artisan expertise. Stevely uprooted from Banff and moved to Oliver, buying land just off Highway 97 at the base of McIntyre Bluff at the north end of town.

Aside from the regulatory hurdles of acquiring a distillery licence, there were building permits and other labyrinthine challenges, but he persevered. And when the provincial liquor laws finally changed to allow breweries and distilleries to have on-site lounges or tasting rooms and, most importantly, to allow products distilled in BC from 100 percent BC raw materials to be sold without the 167 percent tax markup they were previously saddled with, he benefitted along with all other distilleries.

Stevely recognized early on that he couldn't *just* make whisky due to the length of time it takes to age, so he chose to open Dubh Glas Distillery (pronounced "Douglas," which is also his middle name) with a gin. The first batch of Noteworthy Gin came out in February 2015, and it received immediate attention from gin aficionados and cocktail experts, such as Kelowna's Gerry Jobe (see page 144). Stevely chose his botanical mix carefully, opting for a juniper with oaky subtlety rather than the usual juniper that can sear through the other botanicals. The open-concept distillery building and tasting room that Grant designed

Grant Stevely

opened in April 2015. The 79-gallon (300-litre) copper pot Arnold Holstein still from Germany sits right behind the central tasting bar. At the time of writing, fans of Noteworthy Gin are anxiously awaiting the release of Dubh Glas single malt whisky.

Doug and Dawn Lennie

LEGEND DISTILLING

3005 Naramata Road, Naramata | 778-514-1010 | legenddistilling.com

Well, this could be dangerous. Down the road from my house, there is now an excellent craft distillery. DAWN AND DOUG LENNIE started drawing up plans for a distillery as they were selling their wildly popular Bench Market café and fine foods market to Stewart and Heather Glynes in 2013 (see page 191), and Doug was getting out of the construction business. The Lennies bought a cinderblock building that was the Naramata doctor's office and quickly went about remodelling it, acquiring a gleaming copper pot still and 20-plate column and navigating the regulations of opening Naramata's first craft distillery. By July 2014, they were pouring samples of Shadow in the Lake Vodka and Doctor's Orders Gin in their gorgeous tasting room, which looks out through ponderosa pines toward the lake and across to Summerland. The creamy vodka is unfiltered and has pleasing vanilla and caramel notes, maybe from the high-quality Peace Country, BC, wheat that they mash, ferment, and then distill on-site. Local ingredients play an even larger role in the gin. Lavender, apples, juniper berries, elderberries, and mint are combined with coriander and citrus for a complex gin inspired by the view. Bit by bit, they are expanding their line. Backyard Beans coffee is infused into Legend's vodka along with raw cocoa nibs, pure vanilla extract, and demerara sugar for 375 mL bottles of Legend's Blasted Brew. And my personal favourites: the Slowpoke bottles, vodka infusions of Naramata sour cherries, Okanagan apricots, and rhubarb and honey—ready-made local cocktails. I love that, for those who don't drink alcohol, Legend always has an interesting no-booze tipple on tap in the tasting room, from a sarsparilla bitter to a wild rosehip or lavender bitter made with botanicals from Forest Green Man Lavender farm just down the road in Naramata Village.

MAPLE LEAF SPIRITS

948 Naramata Road, Penticton | 250-493-0180 | mapleleafspirits.ca

ANETTE ENGEL tells me that people in Southern Germany are really resourceful to the point where "your neighbour will come after you if you throw out an apple!" She's only half-kidding. So when she and her husband, JORG ENGEL, immigrated to Canada in 2001 and settled in Penticton, they took note of all the local fruit that wasn't being used, essentially going to waste. "We didn't know anything about alcohol regulations here," says Anette, but "coming from Southern Germany, a region with 22,000 small distilleries," it wasn't a total leap to consider making something out of all that ripe fruit. They incorporated in 2004 and became the second licensed distillery in the Okanagan just a few weeks after Okanagan Spirits got its licence in Vernon. They soon struck up a friendship with Okanagan Spirits' founder Frank Deiter, learning what they could as they went. Those early days had their challenges as the regulations around distillation were somewhat archaic. "We had to be in an industrial area because distilling was classified as manufacturing," laughs Anette. The tasting room opened in 2006 in the same building as Jorg's cabinetry busi-ness—an odd pairing, but the arrangement worked out as the latter provided the cash flow for their new undertaking. "The distillery is a very expensive hobby," says Jorg, "even now."

To capitalize on the new tasting room and sales legislation in BC that came into effect in 2013, Jorg and Anette bought a vineyard and home on the well-travelled wine route along Naramata Road across from Red Rooster and Ruby Blues wineries. In July 2014, Maple Leaf Spirits' new tasting room and distillery opened in its much more accessible and scenic location. It is currently the sole distillery in the region distilling only fruit, no grains. They've always had a following with the European crowd in the Okanagan, both tourists and locals, but now with the premium location, they're definitely on the map, and rightly so.

Anette and Jorg Engel

"Here I've got a beautiful bin of export-quality cherries," Anette tells me. "It's just a bit over-ripe, or a stem is broken or missing," noting that a broken stem renders a cherry unshippable to the premium Asian export market. That's the kind of fruit that Maple Leaf Spirits snaps up and distills. Or they pick their own quince for a traditional Swiss dessert liqueur. Their Aged Italian Prune eau-de-vie won a gold medal at the Destillata awards in Vienna, Austria, in 2013. And their Skinny Pinot Noir, one of Jorg's Okanagan grappas, won Spirit of the Year at the 2008 Destillata competition. Maple Leaf Spirits' name comes from the Engels' most popular creation, a maple syrup–infused product built on their cherry-based spirit. It's not as sweet as you might think, and it starts with a distinct maple aroma and finishes with a clean, clear kirsch. Anette's favourite is their Pear Liqueur, in which Bartlett juice is added to a Pear Williams spirit base—fall pear flavour trapped in a bottle.

COURTESY OF NARAMATA CIDER COMPANY / DANIEL SÉGUIN

Del and Miranda Halladay

NARAMATA CIDER COMPANY

Naramata | 778-514-1977 | naramatacider.com

DEL AND MIRANDA HALLADAY are the visionary winemakers who brought major respect to fruit wines with their excellent Elephant Island Orchard Wines, opened in 1999. They eventually added a couple of grape wines to their label a few years back (also excellent). In 2014, they made a few test batches of apple and pear cider that—to no one's surprise—sold out "very quickly." By spring 2015, they were launching a new venture, Naramata Cider Company, in partnership with BRIAN SELWOOD, owner of the Naramata Store. They increased production in 2015, but still can't keep pace with demand for their four crisp, beautifully balanced ciders (Dry Pear, Dry Apple, Apple, and Cider Maker's Select). "We've created this monster," laughs Del.

"It goes back to the heritage of Naramata," says Miranda, referring to the village's legacy as a major apple sorting, packing, and shipping centre. "We build our businesses on what we have already growing here," she says when I ask her whether they use traditional cider apples in their secret blend: "No!" But that's as much as they'll divulge. As with their fruit wines, their philosophy is "not to get hung up on traditional fruit" but to reinvent a modern style that really speaks to local history and place. Naramata Cider Company is currently operating with a mobile cider cart as a pop-up at farmers' markets and other events (private bookings are available). The short-term goal, however, is to secure a permanent Naramata home with a new cidery and tasting room. Of course, bottles are always available at the Naramata Store (225 Robinson Avenue), the heartbeat of the village.

OLD ORDER DISTILLING CO.

270 Martin Street, Penticton | 778-476-2210 | oldorderdistilling.ca

GRAHAM MARTENS can trace his family's history seven generations back to what was then Southern Russia, where his Mennonite ancestors farmed before having to pick up and move over and over again to avoid military service (Mennonites are pacifists). There's been farming in each generation ever since, and Martens grew up on the family's small apple orchard in Summerland. His Old Order Distilling Co., Penticton's newest and only urban distillery, located right in the downtown core, is a nod to his ancestors, the Old Order Mennonites, who hewed to handmade and traditional ways of living, and to the fact that a distilling sideline often went hand in hand with farming in Mennonite communities.

Martens first became intrigued by distilling when he was looking into how to diversify the family orchard business. "My wife"—NAOMI GABRIEL, a member of the Penticton Indian Band—"was really the driver of this business. I'm more of the dreamer," he recounts. "She said, 'Quit talking about it and just do it.'" In May 2014, they hung an "Opening Soon" banner on a shopfront in downtown Penticton and began to really launch themselves into the business, renovating the space, acquiring a German copper still, and applying for permits, despite both having day jobs. (Martens is a fisheries biologist and Gabriel works in finance for the Penticton Indian Band.)

As soon as they got the go-ahead to begin production in November 2014, Martens started experimenting, distilling, and bottling in order to have the tasting lounge and distillery open by April 2015. His malt comes from Gambrinus Malting in Armstrong, and in accordance with craft distillery requirements, he uses 100 percent BC agricultural products to make his base alcohol, Old Order's triple-distilled Heritage Vodka. This is also the base for the Legacy Gin. Martens points out that any vodka, gin, or whisky is about 40 percent alcohol, so "sixty percent of what you're drinking is water." He uses Miller Springs mineral water from Anarchist Mountain, near Osoyoos, as the 60 percent component of

Naomi Gabriel and Graham Martens

his products, because the mineral content and the quality of the water are in keeping with a premium, local spirit product. Eventually he plans to use only local Okanagan desert botanicals in his gin to make a truly Okanagan gin, but for now, he sources local juniper, sumac, and sage and adds distilled Okanagan apples among the aromatics.

The whisky is already in sherry barrels awaiting its requisite "three years and a day" oak barrel residency. (It will be on sale in 2018.) "The question always is," pauses Martens, "how much whisky can you afford to put away?"

SUMMERLAND HERITAGE CIDER COMPANY

3113 Johnson Street, Summerland | 778-738-1155 | summerlandcider.com

The recent boom in apple cider got me thinking about the fact that traditional apple cider requires cider apples. They're the old forgotten "bittersweet" or "bittersharp" varieties that are generally inedible as fresh fruit because they are so tannic, bitter, sweet, or just plain awful-tasting right off the branch. Known in the apple industry as "spitters," because you take a bite and immediately spit it out, they add complexity and character to cider as opposed to a sweet, fizzy, alcoholic apple juice. Apples with names like Yarlington Mill, Harry Masters Jersey, Kingston Black, and Porter's Perfection are now a rarity, though three Summerland apple growers are aiming to turn that around.

About 20 years ago, RON VOLLO, TOM KINVIG, AND BOB THOMPSON started getting together on Tuesdays; they don't remember why they chose Tuesdays, but they'd meet socially and try ciders. Kinvig, in particular, was keen on making homemade cider, curious as to whether he could make something out of his crop of commercial "dessert apples" (the type we buy for eating or cooking) that didn't make the cut to the packing house. The results were "highly variable," and "some were less than good," says Thompson. They weren't entirely put off by the idea, though. They started to collect a few scions—small branches from cider trees they could graft onto mature apple trees—here and there. "We'd literally get one or two scions, and we'd graft them onto a tree," says Thompson. They'd wait until that graft produced other scions, and over the years they finally had enough of the cider wood to produce a sufficient quantity of apples for their small production lots.

They feel the term *microcidery* may be too generous given their small production, yet in 2011, Summerland Heritage Cider Company was able to launch a boutique commercial cidery. Tuesday's Original, fittingly,

COURTESY OF SUMMERLAND HERITAGE CIDER COMPANY

Tom Kinvig, Bob Thompson, and Ron Vollo

was the first label released. It's a classic crisp, off-dry, English-style cider with a 7.7 percent kick. The full-bodied Porter's Dry is made with 100 percent cider apples, while Sweet Paradise has some Jonagold, a dessert apple, for a lighter, slightly sweeter taste.

YOU MIGHT ALSO LIKE

BAD TATTOO BREWING COMPANY brews a good, seasonal beer, like their amber lager, and even Belgian-style ales at this brewhouse restaurant. Look for the giant grain silo just off Lakeshore Drive in downtown Penticton. (169 Estabrook Avenue, Penticton, 250-493-8686, badtattoobrewing.com)

PAUL CECCONI

Brodo Kitchen | 483 Main Street, Penticton | 778-476-1275 | tastebrodo.com

PAUL CECCONI says he's been in professional kitchens since the age of 12. He started with an afterschool job in junior high sweeping up and cleaning pans in a North Vancouver bakery. He kept up this routine of school and work from September to June through high school and would spend his summers waterskiing. After high school, he took culinary arts classes at a Vancouver community college and spent the next six and a half years working his way up in the kitchen at the Four Seasons Hotel in Vancouver, becoming a Red Seal chef in the process. The hotel chain offered a transfer to Sydney, Australia, so Cecconi was on staff when the Four Seasons Sydney was the host hotel for the International Olympic Committee during the 2000 summer games. In 2001, Cecconi was hours away from leaving for his next cooking post, the Four Seasons Nevis in the Caribbean, when the September 11 attacks occurred. Deciding to stay closer to home, he took a job as the sous-chef at the Harvest Golf Club in Kelowna in 2002, becoming the executive chef in 2004 until 2009.

I first met Cecconi when he took on the role of executive chef at Local Lounge and Grille in Summerland. He made it a favourite with residents and tourists with his playful takes on local dishes, ingredients, and menus. But owning his own place was in the back of his mind, so after four years at Local Lounge, Cecconi and his wife, Holly, took over a restaurant on Main Street in Penticton and brought Brodo Kitchen to life in May 2013. It was an immediate hit with its back-to-basics scratch soups, salads, and sandwiches, like the hearty tortilla chicken soup and the three-cheese and Fraser Valley ham grilled cheese. The menu is focused, but Cecconi's creativity gets to shine with the daily features. "It's like coming to my house for dinner," he says. "Too many choices on a menu scare me, as a chef. On a big menu, you know that not everything is going to be fresh."

COURTESY OF BRODO KITCHEN

Paul and Holly Cecconi

Cecconi has the privilege of walking out the restaurant's front door on Saturdays and shopping the Penticton Farmers' Market for ingredients and inspiration. It's what he still loves most about cooking, the excitement of a really great product at its peak of flavour. I'm a huge fan of Brodo's fresh-pressed juices of the day, like strawberry-basil lemonade or lavender lemonade, which capture the essence of the season in a cold, icy glass.

DANA EWART AND
CAMERON SMITH

Joy Road Catering | Penticton | 250-493-8657 | joyroadcatering.com

Every spring, the dates of Joy Road Catering's Alfresco Vineyard Dinners and Winemaker's Dinner Series, which take place on a bluff overlooking Skaha Lake at God's Mountain Estate, are announced. By June, seats are hard to come by—for good reason. For a decade now, chefs DANA EWART and CAMERON SMITH have been at the leading edge of the Okanagan's culinary movement of *cuisine du terroir*. The menus are written for one event only, because it's not about what is in season from their network of foragers, farmers, and other suppliers, but what is ready to eat and at its peak *that day*. At one memorable meal at God's Mountain, as the sun warmed our backs, I marveled at the chilled cucumber and buttermilk soup with tiny cubes of minced Espelette peppers, cherry tomatoes, and emerald green basil. Each course began with either Smith or Ewart listing off the names of the farmers of each ingredient in the dish in front of us. In this case, the Wild Goose Riesling came from the vineyard just a few hundred metres away.

Ewart studied at Stratford Culinary School and cooked at various restaurants in her hometown of Kingston, Ontario. Smith went to George Brown College Chef School in Toronto. They met while working at the same kitchen, Avalon (now closed) in Toronto, and then went on to work with and learn from some of Canada's best chefs—Jamie Kennedy and Normand Laprise. With every penny they saved, they travelled, spending their money on Michelin three-star dinners while staying in hostels. They tucked away taste memories and ideas for when they would have their own kitchen.

In 2005, they arrived to explore the Okanagan. They reconnected with Heidi Noble, a chef-turned-winemaker friend who had just opened JoieFarm Winery with her then husband, Michael Dinn. JoieFarm was offering patio dinners and a farmhouse cooking school, so Smith and Ewart

COURTESY OF JOY ROAD CATERING

Cameron Smith and Dana Ewart

pitched in for a few weeks. Then they cooked briefly at the Bench Market and formulated a plan that would allow them to set up on a shoestring budget and Joy Road Catering was born. Ewart bakes incredible long-ferment artisan sourdough loaves, and makes highly addictive seasonal fruit galettes for their booth at the Penticton Farmers' Market; look for the crowd. And two nights a week during the summer they put on longtable outdoor dinners built around the Okanagan's best ingredients and wines.

A few years ago, they started to raise their own heritage pigs and laying hens. It's an approach to sustainability that permeates everything Joy Road Catering does. The pigs put on weight during the spring, summer, and fall right when the kitchen has loads of scraps and leftovers to deal with. The chickens provide eggs exactly during the months that Ewart and Smith use several dozen per week. At the end of the season, the pigs go to slaughter and become next season's housemade charcuterie and sausages.

"Living the seasons," as Smith says, is a type of commitment that demands a lot of themselves and their team of cooks. There are no shortcuts. And with every mouthful, I'm thankful to Ewart and Smith for going that distance and reconnecting us with the land and the people that make up the Okanagan culinary community.

Carolyn Tipler of Le Petit Clos farm with Lee Humphries

LEE HUMPHRIES

Vintage Hospitality | Black Hills Estate Winery | 4190 Black Sage Road, Oliver
250-498-6606 | blackhillswinery.com

Liquidity Bistro | 4720 Allendale Road, Okanagan Falls | 778-515-5500 | liquiditywines.com

The Sonora Room at Burrowing Owl Estate Winery | 500 Burrowing Owl Place (off Black
Sage Road), Oliver | 250-498-0620 | burrowingowlwine.ca

LEE HUMPHRIES is a soft-spoken man, except when he starts talking about living and cooking in the Okanagan Valley. "It's everything I've wanted to get out of cooking in my life! You can get true farm-to-table here in a way that you can't get in places like Vancouver, even." He would know, having crossed the Atlantic after six-plus years cooking in top London restaurants in his native UK to be the executive chef at FigMint Restaurant (now closed) and to work in prestigious Vancouver establishments like West with David Hawksworth and at Opus Hotel. Humphries joined the team at Robert Clark's C Restaurant in 2010, and by 2012, he was executive chef. In 2013, he had had enough of the big city.

He landed in the Okanagan, first as executive chef at Local Lounge Grille in Summerland. This is where I first experienced his ingredient-first cooking, of course with a garnish of confidence and style from all those years in top kitchens. His food seems effortless, which obviously it's not, but he admits that the immediacy and quality of agriculture here allow him to get back to his roots. Coming from a farm in southwest England, he loves being surrounded with farmers, foragers, and fishers. "This is how I grew up."

Now he's the director of culinary operations at Vintage Hospitality, an Oliver-based restaurant group that runs the Sonora Room at Burrowing Owl Estate Winery, Liquidity Bistro at Liquidity Winery, the kitchen at Black Hills Estate Winery, and even the Gunbarrel Saloon at Apex Mountain Resort. Humphries will now be overseeing teams of chefs, but promises, thankfully, to "keep cooking every day."

DARIN PATERSON

Bogner's of Penticton | 302 Eckhardt Avenue West, Penticton | 250-493-2711 | bogners.ca

When you arrive at Bogner's, a stately old home-turned-restaurant, you pass through chef-owner DARIN PATERSON's raised garden beds thick with fountains of lettuce, kale, rhubarb, and feathery carrot tops. There are also small forests of basil and mint growing in old wine barrels. In addition to over 300 tomato plants in the gardens surrounding the restaurant, there's an abundance of Swiss Chard, kohlrabi, beans, beets, peppers, strawberries, Jerusalem artichokes, garlic, and onions. Paterson is a planter-to-plate chef, and his menus are literally created from the ground up.

Paterson remembers helping out with the vegetable production on the family acreage at the age of seven. By 13 or 14 years old, he was working in restaurant kitchens, and by 18, he flung himself into cooking full time. Highlights from his résumé include four years in the Middle East working for the Saudi royal family before running a high-end catering operation in Stockholm that fed the Nobel Prize recipients, among others. (Both the convivial feel of Middle Eastern cooking and the elegant simplicity of Scandinavian flavours are hallmarks of Paterson's menus.) A 2006 scouting trip for a restaurant in Vancouver took him through the Okanagan Valley, where a heritage house that had been converted into a restaurant was up for sale. He and his family never made it to Vancouver. Bogner's restaurant and catering business keeps him busy, but in the summer, he's even busier with the patio restaurant at nearby Red Rooster Winery.

Darin Paterson

Jenna Pillon

JENNA PILLON

Terrafina at Hester Creek | 887 Road 8, Oliver

250-498-2229 | terrafinarestaurant.com

"I love making people happy through food," says JENNA PILLON, the young, focused, and energetic chef at Terrafina Restaurant at Hester Creek Estate Winery. She did her early culinary training in high school in Salmon Arm, where she was raised. She then took the culinary foundation program at Thompson Rivers University in Kamloops, and then spent a year as a nighttime baker at the Fairmont Chateau Whistler. She continued her culinary arts studies at Okanagan College in Kelowna, completing her Professional Cook Level 3 Apprenticeship in 2011 as a Red Seal chef. While she was working under Paul Cecconi, executive chef at Local Lounge Grille, she entered the 2011 Canadian Culinary Federation's Junior Chef of the Year competition, and won. This earned her a spot at the World Association of Chefs' Societies' Hans Bueschkens Young Chefs Challenge in Las Vegas that year. She finished second overall.

In 2014, Pillon joined the team at Terrafina as sous-chef, but two months later became the restaurant chef—at age 25! The Tuscan-inspired menu at Terrafina plays right into her food sensibility. "I like simple flavours and staying true to the ingredients, but playing with textures and giving them a twist," she says. She draws on her network of suppliers, like Sara Harker from Harker's Organics in Cawston or Jonathan Crofts from Codfathers in Kelowna, and on the restaurant's own herb garden in the back. Its handy for when she's at the centre of the storm during a busy lunch or dinner and can send someone out to pick extra basil or thyme while they feed 200 or so hungry winery guests for a typical July or August lunch.

ADAIR SCOTT

Watermark Beach Resort | 15 Park Place, Osoyoos
watermarkbeachresort.com | 250-495-5500

ADAIR SCOTT was 19 years old when he came to the Okanagan. His first fine-dining experience was in the dining room at the Harvest Golf Club in Kelowna. He returned the very next day, résumé in hand, and said to then-chef Paul Cecconi, "I have to figure out how you did what you did last night." Scott was hired by Cecconi and worked for him for seven years.

"I did my whole apprenticeship with Paul," Scott says. "Every week there were nine or ten farmers coming to the back door." Cecconi would also take Scott along on tours of local farms, which resonated with Scott who grew up on a farm in Prince George.

Scott left Canada to cook for a few years in Australia. When he returned, he felt the pull of the South Okanagan, thanks to some good friends, like Sean and Shannon Peltier, owners of the Lake Village Bakery in Osoyoos (see page 176). Scott was hired as the executive chef at the Watermark Beach Resort, one of the few year-round properties in Osoyoos. The Watermark dining experience is about communal dining, with sharing plates and an outdoor grilling kitchen. Chances are, you'll find the South Okanagan's vegetable and fruit bounty on the menu, but also Okanagan sockeye, caught right in Osoyoos Lake. Scott loves the richness of the South Okanagan foodshed, calling himself a "vege-whereian." "I like to know where my food comes from," he grins.

Adair Scott

DEREK UHLEMANN

Covert Farms | 107th Street, Oliver | 250-498-2731 | covertfarms.ca

At the age of 14, DEREK UHLEMANN applied for a job as a prep cook at the suggestion of his eccentric piano teacher, who noticed that Uhlemann "had clean hands." Uhlemann remembers that he was immediately hooked by the exotic, tactile world of cooking. After a few years in busy kitchens in his late teens, he adventured around as a camp cook in northern BC and travelled to exotic places in the off-seasons—India, Costa Rica, Indonesia, and Mexico—educating his palate. An opportunity to open a wine bar at Silver Star Mountain Resort in Vernon came along in 1999, and he made a daring business decision: 100 percent BC wines. "It was the first list of all BC wines that I had ever seen," he recalls. (*Those* were early days. It took Vancouver a few more years to catch on.) He counts this as his "lucky break," because he met many of the pioneers of the Okanagan wine movement who caused the quality to surge ahead, such as Jeff and Niva Martin of La Frenz, Sandra Oldfield of Tinhorn Creek, and Ian Sutherland at Poplar Grove. "I met David and Cynthia Enns of Laughing Stock Vineyards when they were literally making wine in their garage."

In 2006, Uhlemann and his wife, Sunnie Reinhold, opened Piggy's BarBQ in Penticton. It was my first exposure to excellent pulled smoked pork and barbecued ribs, and it gave me my first taste of Crannóg organic ales from Sorrento, BC. Piggy's closed down in 2008, but once a year, Piggy's roars back to life on Covert Farms in Oliver, where Uhlemann is the farm chef and winery sales manager.

Uhlemann oversees the special events at Covert Farms, a 650-acre certified organic farm on a gorgeous plateau near McIntyre Bluff, one of the most recognizable landmarks in the valley. He raises the herd of Highland cattle, six to eight Berkshire pigs, and Barbados Blackbelly sheep. The livestock breeds were chosen because they're low-intervention animals with few disease issues. The animals are used for meat for the events and for curing in Uhlemann's charcuterie, which is for sale in the

Derek Uhlemann

shop at Covert Farms along with cheeses, other artisan products, and a selection of organic field vegetables and fruits. The farm, which has one of the most popular and extensive U-pick set-ups in the Okanagan, is known for its blueberries, strawberries, and blackberries. It also grows organic bi-coloured corn on the cob, 20 to 30 varieties of tomatoes, six heirloom beet varieties, and onions, peppers, eggplants, watermelons, Athena melons, and other hot-weather ground crops. Some customers just come to buy food to take away or to eat at the picnic tables while enjoying the farm's secluded and picturesque location—oh, and to sample and buy some of Covert Farms' organic, naturally fermented wine.

This is also a certified Salmon-Safe farm, which warrants some explaining. Covert Farms was virgin land when George Covert purchased the farm in 1959. It has been farmed organically, but was using the Okanagan River Channel water to irrigate. An upgrade completed in 1961 allowed the irrigation to come from wells, and the six kilometres (three and a half miles) of river alongside Covert were left untouched by development as original salmon habitat. As the only stretch of the Columbia River system still in its natural state, it's hugely important to the restoration of the Okanagan sockeye and chinook runs here. "That's the advantage of one family holding onto a farm for three generations," says Uhlemann.

Jeff Van Geest

JEFF VAN GEEST

Miradoro at Tinhorn Creek | 537 Tinhorn Creek Road, Oliver | 250-498-3742 | tinhorn.com

"Both of my grandfathers were farmers. And both of my grandmothers were prolific home cooks, bakers, and canners," says JEFF VAN GEEST, executive chef at Miradoro, the sprawling restaurant cantilevered over the vineyards at Tinhorn Creek. His parents helped out on their family farms, as did he while growing up in the produce-rich farmland of the Niagara region of Southern Ontario. The joy of providing good food for people and knowing where the food came from is in his blood.

Van Geest was cooking at Bishop's in Vancouver when visionary restaurateur and chef John Bishop was refining clean, local, seasonal West Coast cuisine and mentoring numerous young chefs, many of whom would go on to become great chefs in their own right. Van Geest opened his own 40-seat Aurora Bistro with his wife, where he continued to hone his own organic, local, and seasonal culinary style. But after five years in Vancouver, they shut the doors on Aurora to look for a calmer pace and real estate they could afford. Luckily, a chef-friend, Derek Uhlemann (now farm chef at Covert Farms in Oliver; see page 242), kept nudging Van Geest to consider the Okanagan. The agricultural vibe and the culinary potential obviously appealed, and Van Geest began with Miradoro in the spring of 2011.

The restaurant hovers out over the vineyard, offering soaring lake views of the South Okanagan. The rustic menus combine just enough culinary craft—like the various handmade pastas, each with their own slightly different dough recipe, or the finishing flourishes on each dish, like salted, cured egg yolk shaved on a risotto—to show off Van Geest's wide-ranging culinary curiosity and a local base of ingredients and products, and, of course, an all-BC wine list, with Tinhorn wines by the glass.

CHRIS VAN HOOYDONK

Backyard Farm Chef's Table | 3692 Fruitvale Way, Oliver

250-485-7749 | backyard-farm.ca

CHRIS VAN HOOYDONK says he now uses the term *work* loosely ever since he made the transition from executive chef to culinary entrepreneur with a farm-to-table lifestyle. "There are no clocks in my kitchen or in the dining room," he says. At 35 years old, he looks even younger, he says he knew that cooking was his calling by the age of 10. Van Hooydonk and his sister often prepared meals together at a young age, helping out their mother, a working single parent. By 17 years old, he was working on his Red Seal chef certification at the Harvest Golf Club in Kelowna, graduating as the apprentice with top marks. By way of cooking stints on a cruise ship, at hotels in Whistler, and at the Four Seasons in Boston, he ended up half a dozen years later as a young executive chef in the dining room of Burrowing Owl Estate Winery.

While Van Hooydonk and his wife were living in the South Okanagan, they rented and eventually purchased an established hobby orchard with about 45 fruit trees. He found he really enjoyed farming, too, and was mentored by a neighbour on adjacent land. Van Hooydonk put together a plan to leave his executive chef job at Burrowing Owl and build a commercial kitchen in his farmhouse's lower level. He opened Artisan Culinary Concepts in June 2013, offering private catering and private culinary workshops. One month later, his neighbour's orchard, with another 60 to 70 old-growth heritage fruit trees and a farmhouse, went up for sale. Van Hooydonk and his wife decided to move ahead more quickly than expected with the next phase of their dream farm, which they had originally planned for five or more years out. He also did all the renovations to the 1924 house, except plumbing and electrical.

Backyard Farm Chef's Table was born, with multi-course, wine-paired culinary demonstrations and events for up to 20 people (private bookings only). Van Hooydonk does all his own butchery and makes his own bread

Chris Van Hooydonk

with his own sourdough starter, which he created by letting his plums hang late on the tree to gather wild yeast to start the fermentation process. He has a handful of favourite produce and meat suppliers and uses what he can from his own orchard farm. Everything is labour-intensive, but it's exactly how he wants to cook. No two meals are ever the same. When he's not creating and serving one-off events, he's working in his orchard. "I have 35- to 50-year-old peach trees that produce one-and-a-half to two-pound peaches. They're absolute juice bombs." He's now shifting the orchards to organic. He picks his fruit only when tree-ripe, and his wife helps pit the fruit, which either gets canned and preserved immediately or cleaned and frozen for the wintertime, when private bookings are slow enough that he can get around to canning. His preserves, such as nectarine and blood orange marmalade, heirloom tomato hot sauces, and cherry-Italian prune plum barbecue sauce, are sold at Covert Farms and Hester Creek Estate Winery.

FARMERS' MARKETS

This information was correct at the time of press, but I've provided web addresses so you can check the hours and locations before you make plans to visit.

NARAMATA COMMUNITY MARKET

1st Street, Wharf Park

Wednesdays, mid-June to early September, 3:30 PM to 6:30 PM

naramatamarket.com

OLIVER FARMERS' MARKET

6607 Station Street, Lion's Park

Thursdays, June to October, 8 AM to 1 PM

exploreoliverbc.com/event/oliver-farmers-market-1

OSOYOOS MARKET ON MAIN

Town Hall Square, Main Street

Saturdays, from the May long weekend to the end of September, 8 AM to 1 PM

Wednesdays, July and August only, 5:30 PM to 8:30 PM

osoyoosmarketonmain.ca

PENTICTON FARMERS' MARKET

100 Block, Main Street

Saturdays, early May to mid-October, 8:30 AM to 1 PM

pentictonfarmersmarket.org

SUMMERLAND SUNDAY MARKET

Main Street

Sundays, third week in June to third week of September, 10 AM to 2 PM

summerlandsundaymarket.ca

THE
SIMILKAMEEN

CAWSTON

HEDLEY

KEREMEOS

SIMILKAMEEN

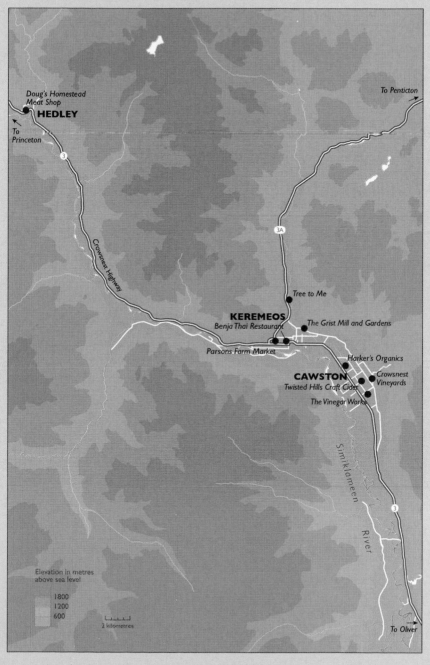

Note that only artisans who welcome visitors on site are shown on this map.

THE SIMILKAMEEN IS A STEEP-SIDED valley that runs for about 200 kilometres (125 miles), following the Similkameen River as it angles southeastward from its headwaters at Manning Park to the village of Cawston and the US border. Home to the Syilx (Okanagan) people for millennia, the hot, fertile valley provided its inhabitants with salmon and trout in its streams and river, game animals and ochre mines in the mountains, and foraging along the valley floor. Settlers arrived in the 1880s for a short-lived gold rush, and others followed to plant the iconic orchards of the region.

The Similkameen is a fraction of the size of its bigger sister next door, the Okanagan Valley, yet it produces fruits, field crops, and wine grapes in abundance with its 2,600 hours of sunlight per year and 181 frost-free days. Lacking large bodies of water like those in the Okanagan Valley, the Similkameen's summer heat is even more extreme and the nights and winters cooler. This produces an intensity of flavour in the fruits and vegetables that is unparalleled in Canada. The valley is home to a small population of farmers, ranchers, bakers, orchardists, winemakers, and a cidermaker, but superlatives abound.

Keremeos is the self-proclaimed "Fruit Stand Capital of Canada," while nearby Cawston trumpets its position as the "Organic Capital of Canada," as 40 percent of the farms in this village are certified organic. While much of the produce (and wine) from this region is available in the Okanagan, you're missing out if you don't meet the food artisans of the Similkameen in person.

THE GRIST MILL AND GARDENS AT KEREMEOS

2691 Upper Bench Road, Keremeos | 250-499-2888 | oldgristmill.ca

CHRIS MATHIESON was 15 years into his career in museums when he became involved in Skipper Otto's Community Supported Fishery (CSF) (skipperotto.com), a direct fisher-to-consumer link where consumers purchase a share each season and then receive quality and sustainably caught local wild fish throughout the season. Skipper Otto's, based in Vancouver, was the first CSF in Canada and second in the world. That experience, Mathieson says, brought a new awareness about food linkages and ideas about food security.

When the Grist Mill and Gardens, the food-focused provincial heritage agricultural site in Keremeos, was looking for a site manager, Mathieson was an ideal fit. He and his family moved to the Similkameen, and he now has a decade-long agreement to manage and run the 12-acre site, which includes, among other things, an orchard with over 40 historical apple varieties, a dozen small plots of heritage wheat varieties, and a water wheel–powered flour mill. His job, he says, is to demonstrate what "history tastes like" for locals and visitors who drop in for a tour, go for lunch at the café, or attend one of the many special events throughout the season. (The Grist Mill is open from the Victoria Day long weekend to the Thanksgiving long weekend.)

Chris Mathieson

One of the the Grist Mill's biggest contributions to Canada's culinary history—no small feat—is its role in the revival of Red Fife wheat. This turn-of-the-last-century wheat, a parent to Marquis wheat, made Canada the bread basket to the world. Yet as "new and improved" varieties, like Marquis, came on the market, Red Fife dropped out of use. In 1988, Grist Mill site managers Sharon Rempel and Cuyler Page began the Heritage Wheat Program. With only a pound of each of seven historic varieties, including Red Fife, they planted small plots and started what became a huge attraction at the Grist Mill. Red Fife, however, was the star. Rempel figured that Red Fife could be revived for commercial use, and by 2006, over 200 tonnes of it were harvested on organic farms across Canada. It is now grown nationwide and is used by artisan bakers because it is ideally suited to traditional sourdough slow-fermented breads. Small independent bakeries, like True Grain Bread, were an important link, as they created demand for Red Fife by turning it into sought-after breads. More interestingly, explains Rempel in "Red Fife Wheat," an article on her website, Grassroot Solutions (grassrootsolutions.com), Red Fife's colour and flavour characteristics are highly influenced by the growing conditions, giving a different bread terroir to Red Fife grown in different parts of the country.

Tree to Me

TREE TO ME

1217 Highway 3A, Keremeos | 250-499-9271 | treetome.ca

JOE WURZ moved to Vancouver for university, and then stayed on for a career. Having grown up in Keremeos, however, he was never satisfied with the quality of produce in the city. Plans to bring quality, organic fruits and vegetables to the urban environment brewed until he eventually acquired 40 acres of farmland. Joe and son SEAN WURZ planted an orchard and learned what produce thrived on the land, gaining organic certification along the way. Then, they built a farm market, which included a bakery and café, along with a B&B featuring suites that make the most of the sweeping valley and mountain views.

Tree to Me opened its doors to the public in 2013 as a year-round agritourism destination in the Similkameen Valley. Joe's son ANDREW WURZ has since joined to run the market and bakery, along with his husband STÉPHANE CANTAVÉNÉRA, who manages the six B&B suites. As the seasons progress, the farm market features ground crops and fruits that are at their peak—peppers, tomatoes, garlic, cauliflower, beets, beans, and more. Over 15 varieties of apples, four types of plums, apricots, peaches, and nectarines come out of the orchard, with cherry trees coming into maturity soon. The recent addition of greenhouses means leafy greens and other vegetables are available throughout the colder months. Housemade jams, jellies, pickles, and preserves are for sale as well as Tree to Me's artisan breads, fruit pies, and meat pies. Organic coffee and casual breakfast and lunch items are available as well. The market also carries its own bath and body product line called Little Luxuries and giftware crafted by local artisans.

THE VINEGAR WORKS

669 Kurtz Road, Cawston | 250-506-0114 | thegarden.ca, thevinegarworks.com

"No matter how hard we tried, we couldn't keep Erik out of agriculture," say KEN AND ELKE KNECHTEL. They have a three-acre nursery greenhouse in Maple Ridge, BC, called Red Barn Plants and Produce, and their son, ERIK KNECHTEL, kept hijacking the greenhouses for his own purposes. The senior Knechtels decided to partner with Erik and buy another farm that Erik would manage. They found a property in Cawston in 2009, and now Erik manages the mix of McIntosh and cider apples, tomatoes, golden watermelon, Stallion White cucumbers and traditional cucumber varieties, a dozen varieties of peppers, sweet potatoes, and culinary herbs, including lemongrass.

The Cawston farm came with four 64-square-foot dryers, likely left over from the 1970s, when fruit leathers were a boom industry in the region. Erik decided to put them back into use, drying garlic scapes, sage, rosemary, thyme, and even hot peppers for a line of dried herb-infused sea salts.

In 2014, the Knechtels bought the Vinegar Works, an established organic vinegar operation started in Summerland in 2000 by John Gordon and Kim Stansfield. Vinegar production was a perfect fit for another dimension to the Cawston farm and ensured that this beloved artisan vinegar product would continue past Gordon and Stansfield's retirement. They happily worked with Erik as the business changed hands. "There were sparks of excitement flying from John," says Ken. "There was Erik, a 25-year-old, asking all the right questions." With the Vinegar Works' established networks already in place for organic grapes, production just continued along, and in 2015, a new building opened with a tasting—or sniffing—room for on-site sales.

Erik Knechtel

YOU MIGHT ALSO LIKE

THE SMOKING GUN PEPPERCORN COMPANY, which Brent McClelland and Ed Vermette started in Princeton in 2004. Infused with everything from bourbon to Shiraz red wine, their whole black peppercorns are surprisingly tasty, with a twist. (250-295-7441, thesmokinggunpepper.com)

SIMILKAMEEN APIARIES

2098 Ritchie Drive, Cawston | 250-499-2555

I first tasted warm honey out of a hive at CHERYL AND BLAIR TARVES's certified organic farm property in the Similkameen. I was on a food tour of farms in a 1.6-kilometre (1-mile) radius of Orofino Winery in Cawston, where we ended up later that day for a sumptuous dinner prepared with ingredients from only this rather small geographic area. Wearing only a T-shirt, shorts, and a tattered Panama hat with a bandana as a hat band—no beekeeper's veil, no white coverall suit, no kid-leather beekeeping gloves—Blair opened the top of a hive with his prybar-like hive tool, puffed some smoke inside to calm the bees, then picked up a frame, brushed the bees away, and invited our group to dig a finger into the warm wax and honey. One by one, we tasted some of the most exquisite honey I've ever had.

Blair's grandfather was an orchardist and beekeeper in Oyama, and Blair became fascinated with the whole process of raising queens, keeping bees, and producing honey from an early age. He took a beekeeping course at Fairview College in Northern Alberta, then spent time in California in the 1980s because, "at the time, the best beekeepers in the world were located in Northern California," he says.

When Blair and Cheryl met, they both knew they wanted to be full-time beekeepers. They looked at Pender Island on the West Coast to set up their business, but in the end, the Similkameen had the best climate to raise queens, says Blair. He explains that the all-important mating flight of the queen—one flight through a cloud of drones during which she hopefully mates with 10 to 20 of them—is highly weather-dependent. It only happens if the weather is just right: a nice sunny, warm, windless day. The Similkameen has lots of those in the spring. That said, what makes it a great location for rearing queens and successful mating flights creates challenges for honey production. The narrow Similkameen Valley is hot and dry, and the bees have only about a 60-kilometre (40-mile) gorge to forage in.

Cheryl and Blair Tarves

The honey that Similkameen Apiaries produces from its 200 hives is highly concentrated, low-moisture, multifloral wild flower honey. Each hive produces a mere 27 to 36 kilograms (60 to 80 pounds) per year, whereas a hive in Northern Alberta can produce up to 110 kilograms (250 pounds) or more. Oh, but the flavour. Because of the lower moisture content, honey from the Tarves's bees is thick and spicy with desert aromas. This is why it's a favourite of many chefs in the valley who buy honey from Similkameen Apiaries as well as their exquisite honeycombs—beautiful golden honey suspended in a snow-white beeswax comb, all completely edible and fantastic when paired with a local blue cheese. Rob Walker, executive chef at Liquidity Bistro in Okanagan Falls, makes an incredible honeycomb and vanilla ice cream with the Tarves's honeycomb and honey.

Cheryl and Blair have been fixtures at the Penticton Farmers' Market for the past 24 years, and they are vocal about the fact that they sell honey only from their hives and from their farm—rightfully so, as honey labelling rules are extremely lax and "local honey" isn't always as local as it appears on the jar.

Cheryl and Blair keep about 200 hives for honey production, another 200 for raising queens, and 100 for other products and as backup. In summer, the honey hives are spread through the Similkameen on certified organic farms and wildlands where the bees can collect nectar and pollen from over a dozen different flowering food sources. Such is the magic of small-lot, artisan honey. It expresses the season and the flowers that were blooming when it was collected. And as the seasons change, so, ever so slightly, does the taste of the honey. "Honey has vintages," Blair reminds me.

✕

We really need to talk about the bees. One in three mouthfuls in our food system depends on the work of pollinators. Agriculturally, we depend on European honeybees as the main pollinator for most of our fruit, vegetable, and even seed crops, from asparagus to apples, cauliflower to cantaloupe, strawberries to sunflower seeds. Put that in perspective, and beekeeping isn't just a quaint hobby that produces a sweet end product. Bees, especially honeybees, are a critical part of our food system.

The more I learn about them, the more respect I have for both honeybees and our local beekeepers. I like to think of the Similkameen as the Shangri-La for bees. Cawston, the "Organic Capital of Canada," with 40 percent of farms certified organic and many more organic in practice, is particularly important in light of Colony Collapse Disorder (CCD), a phenomenon that started to occur in 2006, when beekeepers in North America and Europe reported that worker bees were abandoning otherwise viable hives. CCD has been decimating up to a third of European honeybee colonies, and scientific research is zeroing in on neonicotinoids as the cause. They're a class of systemic pesticides that end up in the leaves, fruit, flowers, and pollen of plants; they've been banned in Europe since 2013, but are still used in North America. Not only are bees in the Similkameen not exposed to as many pesticides as other honeybees might be elsewhere, but the relative diversity of farming and natural spaces in the region as a whole gives bees a nice mix of food to forage on throughout the season, not just a monocrop diet. Sure, they have to contend with the notorious Similkameen wind, and bees hate wind, but overall it's a good environment for a bee. In return, we get these incredibly interesting, flavour-layered local honeys from healthy, happy hives.

FARMERSDOTTER ORGANICS

2036 Osprey Lane, Cawston | 250-506-1958 (Holmes)

250-263-1943 (Kosugi) | farmersdotter.ca

"I am a farmer's daughter, and I'm of Swedish ancestry," laughs YVONNE (YVE) KOSUGI, explaining the origins and spelling of Farmersdotter on the labels of her artisan breads, flavoured salts, jams, and—my personal addiction—habañero pumpkin seed brittle. I know her from the Penticton Farmers' Market, but customers in the Cawston area come straight to the farm on baking days.

After years of working in Northern BC, both Kosugi and her partner, MORRIS HOLMES, were easily swayed by Kosugi's half-brother's plea for help in running a fruit stand he was taking over from an uncle. (The half-brother is Quentin Parsons, of Parsons Farm Market in Keremeos; see page 280.) The mild winters and the "southern interior" lifestyle appealed to Kosugi and Holmes, and two years after moving to the Similkameen, they bought a farm property: a seven-acre certified organic garlic farm with excellent soil that ran one metre (three feet) deep (extraordinary for the Okanagan and Similkameen Valleys) and just needed some new, enthusiastic farmers.

Being an avid home baker, Kosugi noted the rather impressive wood-fired oven on the property. Turns out it was built by legendary wood-fired bread-oven maker Alan Scott, and with an interior baking surface of 183 by 244 centimetres (72 by 96 inches), it was designed to bake up to 75 loaves at a time. (For the bread-heads out there, Chad Robertson of Tartine Bakery fame in San Francisco lived on Alan Scott's property, learned to bake bread in a wood-fired oven, and is now the rock star of artisan bread in the US.)

Kosugi now bakes three batches on Fridays to keep up with the demand at the Penticton Farmers' Market for her five different loaves. She uses only natural leavener, a living, breathing sourdough starter, for her breads and occasional Montreal-style wood-fired bagels. Her most

Yvonne Kosugi

popular is the Similkameen Sourdough, which contains both organic white and rye flours. Flax to the Max is a hearty loaf with incredible nutty flavours from a high concentration of ground flax. (Kosugi's mother is a certified organic grain grower in Saskatchewan, and she sends Kosugi large quantities of flax.) The Seeded Honey Rye is chock full of sunflower seeds, pumpkin seeds, flax, oats, and honey from neighbouring Similkameen Apiaries. Olive and Rosemary is a sourdough with a Mediterranean personality. And the highly addictive Farmhouse Focaccia features herbs from the farm and Kosugi's crunchy garlic scape salt, Farmersdotter's current runaway hit.

Holmes tends the 100,000 organic garlic plants, and Kosugi points out that "it's all hand-done growing"—meaning on hands and knees to plant, weed, and pick the sixteen 180-metre- (600-foot-) long rows. In 2014, they had the idea to make infused sea salts, including one featuring garlic scapes, those looping flower stalks of hardneck garlic varieties that can be harvested while the garlic continues to grow throughout the summer. In 2015, they had to increase production because they just couldn't keep the salts in stock. Kosugi has also been experimenting with smoked and spiced versions using her brother's dried habañero chilies.

TWISTED HILLS CRAFT CIDER

2080 Ritchie Drive, Cawston | 250-488-4256 | twistedhills.ca

"It's the craft cider revolution," KAYLAN MADEIRA tells me as we ponder the number of new cideries opening in the Okanagan and Similkameen. "But nobody has the number of varieties and the supply that we have," she states.

When they bought their seven-acre organic orchard in Cawston, Madeira and her husband, JO SCHNEIDER, decided to plant a wide variety of French and English cider apples, including Calville Blanc d'Hiver, Kingston Black, and Cox's Orange Pippin. At first they grew for other ciderhouses. Then, in 2011, they started to make small batches of their own cider for friends and family, who encouraged them to keep brewing and think about launching their own label. Inspired by the quality artisan cideries on Vancouver Island, like Sea Cider Farm and Ciderhouse in Saanichton, they decided that they could establish a premium craft cider with the excellent organic fruit they already produced. They enrolled in a cidermaking course in Washington, and in 2013, they began what would be their first commercial batches of cider. "It's a year-long process. The orchard is always in constant need of something!" says Madeira, from pruning in the winter months to budbreak and blossoming in the spring, to picking in the fall.

Schneider and Madeira pick each apple variety only as it achieves the right levels of acidity and sugar. Some apples are picked in late August and some as late as early October. The fruit that goes into each blend, however, is crushed at the same time throughout October. Fermentation takes a few months, and the yeast is removed as it is spent and settles. The cider is allowed to mature at a cool temperature before they bottle and pasteurize each variety throughout March and April, right as the orchard is waking up again and budding out into blossom for the next crop of fruit and the next batch of ciders.

Madeira knows the start-up's 10- by 5-metre (32- by 16-foot) tasting room can get a bit tight. "We do everything in here," she says, but you

Jo Schneider and Kaylan Madeira

can also see what goes into making craft cider. Twisted Hills' four hard ciders—Kingston's Twist, Calville's Winter, Pippin's Fate, and Tangled Rose—and one sparkling non-alcoholic variety are all made from 100 percent certified organic fruit from their farm. The cidery is a great pet- and kid-friendly spot, with an orchard picnic area to relax in during the heat of the day.

Sascha Heinecke

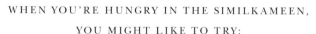

WHEN YOU'RE HUNGRY IN THE SIMILKAMEEN,
YOU MIGHT LIKE TO TRY:

BENJA THAI RESTAURANT, for some seriously good Thai food that is made by
hand with care by the Chaicomdee family, who immigrated to Canada from
Thailand in 1989 and settled in the valley. (516 7th Avenue, Keremeos,
250-499-2561, benjathairestaurant.com)

CROWSNEST VINEYARDS, for traditional German fare (Bratwurst! Schnitzel!
Rouladen!) in the dining room or on the outdoor patio, and to stock up
on European-style breads made in the wood-fired oven (which winery
chef Sascha Heinecke also uses to make excellent pizza). There's also
an on-site guesthouse if you want to stay the night. (2035 Surprise Drive,
Cawston, 250-499-5129, crowsnestvineyards.com)

Wilfrid and Sally Mennell

AMBROSIA APPLES

Cawston | ambrosiaapples.com

Ambrosia apple trees in Chile, Italy, New Zealand, Australia, and the US all owe their existence to what WILFRID MENNELL describes as his negligence. "If I'd have been doing my weeding properly, I would have ripped it out," he says of the little sapling that had grown between the rows of Jonagold apples on SALLY MENNELL's 12-acre orchard in Cawston. (Married with children and grandchildren, Wilfrid and Sally each have their own organic orchard. Perhaps the secret to a long, happy marriage is separate orchards, about a mile apart.)

By the time they noticed the sapling, they decided it should stay. When the tree was old enough to produce fruit in 1990, the pickers working in that orchard had stripped it clean, eating every apple. That's when the Mennells really knew that they had something special. "In 1991, we began to test it," says Wilfrid. He took buds—the precursors to new shoots—from this interesting new tree and grafted them onto existing apple trees to ensure that the cuttings would grow into fruiting branches and would carry the same characteristics of the original tree. Finally, they sent a few sample apples to an organic fruit broker that Wilfrid's brothers worked with. "He wanted to know how many pallets I had to sell!"

The Mennells spent the next few years learning about plant breeders' rights as well as the intricacies of developing and marketing a new variety. They worked with the newly formed Okanagan Plant Improvement Corporation to register this new apple and began to license it to other growers. "I don't know if you can imagine the excitement of standing in a five-acre orchard of Ambrosia in New Zealand," Wilfrid says proudly. He and Sally have met all of the orchardists who have an exclusive licence to grow this apple, from Chile to Australia. Now millions of Ambrosia apples are grown around the world, from one seedling on an organic orchard in Cawston.

FOOD OF THE SUN

395 VLA Road, Cawston | 250-506-003

Considering the Similkameen's searing summer heat, I'm constantly impressed with the salad greens and tender herbs that JUSTENE WRIGHT AND MATT LOUGHEED grow on their certified organic Cawston farm. Their stall at the Penticton Farmers' Market has an impressive array of several salad greens, lots of spinach in the early spring, arugula, Asian greens, kale, broccoli, cauliflower, mustard greens, cucumbers, dill, cilantro, and more. Wright says she focuses on greens, no matter the challenges, because that's what she most loves to eat. She also has a third of an acre planted in Russian Red garlic and an early Asian variety.

Wright grew up in Calgary, and it was only when she was working at Sunnyside Natural Market, an independent grocery store in Calgary's Kensington neighbourhood, that she came to hear of the Similkameen. "I made friends with those farmers [whose products were sold at Sunnyside], and they always had a twinkle in their eye," she says.

When Wright's sister bought an orchard in Keremeos, Wright paid her a visit. After meeting a farmer who needed some help in her garlic field, Wright decided on the spot that she'd try her hand at farming and leave the big city behind. She then met her partner, Matt Lougheed, who had grown up in the Similkameen, and they farmed on leased land for four years. In 2012, they purchased their own property. "It totally changed our lives," says Wright.

Wright sells only at the Penticton Farmers' Market and through her 22-week Community Supported Agriculture (CSA) program. She likes to keep the scope of her farm narrow, focusing on the quality of the vegetables and greens and only on what she really loves. "I have this passion about soil health and about the fact that what I grow has really dense nutrients," she says. The minerality of the soil in the Similkameen really comes through in her vegetables and greens, so, difficult or not to grow them, I'm glad she does.

Justene Wright and Matt Lougheed

Sara Harker

HARKER'S ORGANICS

2238 Highway 3, Cawston | 250-499-2751 | harkersorganics.com

Over the past 128 years, five generations of the Mannery/Harker family have been farming the same land in the Similkameen Valley. They have raised dairy cows and beef cattle and grown ground crops and tree fruits. In fact, you can still visit the Snow apple tree (also known as the Fameuse variety and a parent to the McIntosh variety) that was planted back in 1916. (Happy 100th birthday, Snow Fameuse!)

In 1961, the third generation on the land, Ken and Marjorie Harker, opened an on-farm retail market. The fourth generation, Bruce and Kathy Harker, built a wholesale packing house on the property to pack fruit for other growers in the area. When Bruce and Kathy's kids, JASON, TYLA, TROY, AND ALYSHA HARKER, took the reins, the fifth generation decided to return to a sustainable model in organics. Now Harker's is a 30-acre organic farm that grows vegetables and tree fruits and has an on-farm retail market, a packing house for 30 other organic growers in the Similkameen, and an excellent certified organic fruit winery under its own label, Rustic Roots. The farming is still done largely by Bruce and Troy, with 12 acres of tree fruits and 15 acres of vegetables. Troy runs the fruit packing, brokering, and selling. He also helps out in the winery and cellar, where his wife, SARA HARKER, is the winemaker (and maker of a delicious sparkling hard cider called Rustic Roots' Snow Cider). Sara also manages the retail store and coordinates the fruit and vegetable orders from and deliveries to the 30 restaurants they supply in the valley, from Osoyoos to Kelowna.

Strong advocates for organics in the Similkameen, the Harkers are committed to the extra work it entails, taking a long view of the farm's health and productivity. "Protecting our farm's little ecosystem is a matter of sustainability," says Sara. "We want something that we'll have for the next generation." Bruce and Kathy have eight grandkids, some of whom live on the farm, so it looks like that next generation will be ready to step into the family business in due time.

HONEST FOOD FARM

2305 Ferko Road, Cawston | 250-499-5381

Honest Food Farm's stand has such a big presence and such a wide variety of vegetables at the Penticton Farmers' Market, I ask BRANDIE ZEBROFF how they can have such a relatively small farm in Cawston. She and her husband, YURI ZEBROFF, farm five acres that they own in Cawston and another seven acres that they lease nearby on the edge of Keremeos, yet they grow and sell pretty much everything that can grow in the region, from asparagus to zucchini. Brandie laughs and simply says, "Yuri is an extreme organic farmer."

Yuri's parents, GEORGE AND ANNA ZEBROFF, were pioneering organic farmers in the Similkameen in 1972. "Things were different then. They used to pretend to spray," Brandie says, just to keep the neighbours at bay. Brandie grew up in Cawston, but never dreamed she'd end up farming. After she met Yuri, they worked on his parents' orchard for 12 years before leasing land to farm organic vegetables, eventually buying it in December 2008. This clearly was not motivated by profit or lifestyle—growing organic vegetables must be the most physically demanding farming decision anyone could make—but because they "just wanted to grow good food for people to eat." They also wanted an environment where their kids could run through the orchard and fields whenever they wanted and eat whatever they wanted without worrying about the timing of the last spray.

They're extremely committed to providing good, clean food directly to people in the Okanagan. "I hope for a time when everybody has access to all these great products that we have in this valley," Brandie says. Having patiently waited for their fruit trees to mature, they are now producing apricots, cherries, peaches, nectarines, apples, plums, and pears. They are known for their delicious heirloom tomatoes and particularly potent, flavourful garlic. The combination of the valley-bottom soil and the intense heat of the Similkameen results in a special

Brandie and Yuri Zebroff

growing environment in Canada, says Brandie. The heat is challenging physically for farmers, "but the melons and tomatoes need that heat to ripen. I don't know that there's another place like ours in Canada."

While finding farming help isn't easy, they have made a go of it and have been able to raise three children without off-farm income. This isn't the norm for small family farms in Canada, but it comes with its own rewards, says Brandie. "We work on the land. We get dirty. At the end of the day, we enjoy good food and drink."

PARSONS FARM MARKET

110 7th Avenue, Keremeos | 250-499-2312 | parsonsfarmmarket.wordpress.com

In 1908, QUENTIN PARSONS's great-grandfather planted his first orchard block of apples in Keremeos. And in 1948, Parsons's great-uncle opened the Similkameen's first fruit stand as traffic began to increase on Highway 3. Soon afterwards, Parsons's grandfather opened a fruit stand, and so did another great-uncle. "At one point, there were three Parsons Fruit Stands in Keremeos!" laughs Parsons. Over a century since that first planting of apples, the farm and his great-uncle's initial fruit stand are still there, though the competition is much stiffer in the Fruit Stand Capital of Canada, says Parsons, who took over the family business in 2008.

Although living in Vancouver at the time, Parsons had always maintained a connection to the farm and the fruit stand, mostly by coming out to Keremeos as a teenager to work in the fruit stand. "A lot of the farming aspects don't come naturally for me," he admits, though he seems to be doing a fine job. The fruit stand continues to thrive in the competitive seasonal market, and many chefs in the valley cook with his vegetables thanks to a small-scale distribution network called Seasons Harvest, out of Kelowna, which brings his 65 varieties of tomatoes, 12 varieties of eggplant, 12 varieties of cucumbers, and exotic Asian herbs to them and to chefs in Vancouver, Banff, and Calgary. The multi-generational orchards he now tends produce nine varieties of apricots as well as cherries, apples, plums, peaches, pears, and nectarines. While he's low-key about his growing methods, they are essentially organic in practice, though his 10-acre farm is not fully certified organic. "I don't cut any corners with chemical fertilizers or chemical sprays," he says, adding that he does farm another five acres in Cawston that are certified organic.

Parsons and his partner, STEFANIE SCHULTZE, are building a line of unique value-added products like cherry-basil juice, apricot-habañero-lime jam, and apple chips with chai masala spice. He loves the creative

Quentin Parsons and Stefanie Schultze

aspects of the crazy mix of a life that is farming and retailing direct to chefs and consumers. It's also about keeping his family's business alive. "You won't survive at all if you aren't doing something that keeps you competitive."

Brent McClelland

DOUG'S HOMESTEAD MEAT SHOP

6245 Highway 3, Hedley | 250-292-8364 | dougshomestead.com

Doug's Homestead Meat Shop is, frankly, in the middle of nowhere, but owners BRENT AND LINETTE MCCLELLAND note that they sell over 140 kilograms (300 pounds) of their beef jerky alone every day through the front door. (They receive email orders from places like New Jersey, Japan, and Costa Rica, but they're not interested in international shipping.) Many, and I mean many, make the trip for the love of really, really great beef jerky, smoked baby back ribs, pork sausage, and freshly ground hamburger patties. The smoker runs all day, but arrive early, because it's common for the shop to be out of jerky by mid-afternoon.

The McClellands—who bought the shop in 2007 and kept the original name—say the original owner, Doug, is still a regular, reliable customer.

FARMERS' MARKETS

Because the Similkameen has so many fruit stands and farm-gate stores, there are no farmers' markets *per se*.

Check out similkameenvalley.com/food/fruit.php for a listing of fruit stands in the area.

RECOMMENDED
RESOURCES

READING

BC Food History Network, based in the Okanagan, is the website to quench your curiosity about the region's culinary history. Browse the resources, classroom curricula, and research at bcfoodhistory.ca.

Looking for a fruit recipe or information about fruit ripening times, varieties, and local fruit farmer profiles? BC Tree Fruits has it covered at bctree.com.

Real Food, Real Health: A Guide to Finding, Preparing, and Enjoying Local Foods by MAUREEN CLEMENT and KATHRYN HETTLER (2010), is a fantastic local resource, available as a free PDF download from pilgrimsproduce.com/book. This book contains profiles of several Armstrong-area farmers, dairy farmers, orchardists, and market gardeners. I love the encyclopedic pages on the various local fruits, vegetables, and nuts in the North Okanagan. There are also some great tips on picking out fruit and produce at their peak of ripeness for maximum flavour and nutrition, as well as simple recipes and preserving tips.

With 40-some wineries alone on the Naramata Bench now, GARTH EICHEL's timely and well-researched book *Naramata Bench Vineyards & Wineries* (Archipelago Media, 2015) contains profiles of almost all the winemakers along this scenic strip from Penticton to Okanagan Mountain Park. It contains useful touring, dining, and accommodation listings too.

Award-winning author BERNADETTE MCDONALD and farmer-artist KAROLINA BORN-TSCHÜEMPERLIN teamed up to write and illustrate the beautiful *Okanagan Slow Road* (TouchWood Editions, 2014). It's a great take on two locals' experiences of living the slow life in the valley.

Menus from an Orchard Table: Celebrating the Food and Wine of the Okanagan (Whitecap Books, 2011) is chef-winemaker HEIDI NOBLE's love letter to the ingredients of the Okanagan. It contains menus and recipes developed in the first few years of Joie Winery, now called JoieFarm, when it was a farmhouse dining destination as well as a B&B.

The Field Guide is writer, visual designer, and photographer TARYNN PARKER's online resource guide to the best foods, wines, destinations, and experiences in the Okanagan and Similkameen. Check it out at thefieldguide.ca. *Okanagan: A Celebration of the Canadian Wine Region* (The Field Guide Publishing, 2015) is her gorgeous, photo-filled coffee table book profiling a number of the valley's best winemakers.

JENNIFER SCHELL is the editor of *Wine Trails*, a free, handy quarterly magazine available widely in the Okanagan. She is also the author of beautiful cookbooks that celebrate the people, places, and products of British Columbia. The first edition of *The Butcher, the Baker, the Wine & Cheese Maker: An Okanagan Cookbook* (2012), won a World Gourmand Cookbook Award for Best Local Cuisine Book in Canada. She expanded the series with *The Butcher, the Baker, the Wine & Cheese Maker By the Sea* (TouchWood Editions, 2015). The second edition of *The Butcher, the Baker, the Wine & Cheese Maker In the Okanagan* is being published in 2016 by TouchWood Editions.

Vancouver-based wine writer JOHN SCHREINER has been chronicling the Okanagan and Similkameen wine scene for over a decade. His 15 books— and counting—are excellent resources for their accuracy and concision.

Schreiner even seems to know about wineries that are opening before anyone else. Pick up John Schreiner's *Okanagan Wine Tour Guide: The Wineries of British Columbia's Interior, 5th edition* (Whitecap Books, 2014) for the most up-to-date information on the region's wineries. He maintains a companion blog at johnschreiner.blogspot.ca.

I absolutely love SummerLand Online, this community's web magazine by resident STEPHANIE SEATON. It's a neatly organized website written by locals about local businesses, foods, and recipes. Please visit summerland-online.com.

There's a Slow Food convivium that covers the Thompson Okanagan and works to support and promote "good, clean, and fair" food in the area. You can find events and chapter news at sfto.ca.

LISTENING
The Ruminant is Peachland farmer JORDAN MARR's podcast, in which he digs deep into the issues around small-scale and sustainable agriculture and food culture. Find the podcasts at theruminant.ca.

LUKE WHITTALL's BC Wine Country podcast and blog go "beyond the guided tour of wine in British Columbia" at winecountrybc.wordpress.com. Whittall and colleagues from the Okanagan wine industry are in their fifth season of musings about what really goes on around here.

WATCHING
In 2008, *Tableland*—a 2007 documentary that spans California to BC and features many producers and winemakers from the Okanagan—won Best Feature at the New York City Food Film Festival. Filmed, narrated, and produced by CRAIG NOBLE (JoieFarm winemaker HEIDI NOBLE's brother), it is a beautiful overview of the farm-to-table movement in the valley and in our wider North American culinary community.

VISITING

The local tourism boards in the region have excellent online resources for farms, U-picks, winery routes, accommodations, food and wine events, and other important information for culinary adventurers:

Armstrong: hellobc.com/armstrong.aspx

Kelowna: tourismkelowna.com

Naramata: discovernaramata.com

Oliver: winecapitalofcanada.com

Osoyoos: destinationosoyoos.com

Penticton: visitpenticton.com

Similkameen: similkameenvalley.com

Thompson Okanagan Tourism Association: totabc.org

Vernon: tourismvernon.com

Wines of British Columbia: winebc.com

Here are a few more handy regional websites:

Naramata Bench: naramatabench.com

Okanagan Falls Winery Association: ofwa.ca

Okanagan Wine Festivals (four major wine festivals each year with dozens of events in communities from Big White to Osoyoos): thewinefestivals.com

Oliver Osoyoos Wine Country: oliverosoyoos.com

Summerland's Bottle Neck Drive: bottleneckdrive.com

You'll also find excellent in-person advice on culinary touring (and free maps) at:

BC VQA Wine Information Centre, 553 Vees Drive (corner of Eckhardt Avenue and Highway 97), Penticton, 250-490-2006, pentictonwineinfo.com

British Columbia Visitor Centre @ Osoyoos, 9912 Highway 3 (at the junction of Highways 3 and 97), Osoyoos, 250-495-5410

Kelowna Visitor Centre, 544 Harvey Avenue, Kelowna, 250-861-1515, tourismkelowna.com

Oliver Visitor Centre, 6431 Station Street, Oliver, 778-439-2363, winecapitalofcanada.com

Vernon Visitor Centre, 3004 39th Avenue, Vernon, tourismvernon.com

Send me your favourite resources and events and I'll post them at foodgirl.ca under the "Food Artisans" section and on Facebook at facebook.com/FoodArtisansoftheOkanagan.

ACKNOWLEDGEMENTS

What a pleasure it was to dive into the deep end of the Okanagan's pool of culinary artisans! I wrote this book for all passionate culinary craftspeople of our region, whether you made it into these pages or not. This book merely starts the conversation of our vibrant and exciting culinary community and food scene.

Thanks to all of you who took the time to relay your stories to me and for the excellent products you make and contribute to the Okanagan foodshed.

I owe a huge debt to my friend and food-writing colleague, Roslyne Buchanan (rozsmallfry.com), who contributed greatly with research assistance, ideas, and opinions and is a great road-trip companion and dinner date. Despite having her own deadlines for food and travel stories, Roz provided much-needed clear thinking and cheerleading, two very important elements in getting a book from planning to page. I promise to return the favour one day, Roz.

To the team at TouchWood Editions: Thank you to the astute and ambitious Taryn Boyd, associate publisher at TouchWood Editions and Brindle & Glass Publishing, for bringing me to this project and having such a strong vision for the potential of this book. To my editor, Lana Okerlund, my sincerest appreciation for your role as collaborator to bring this book to life. Thank you for cleaning up my writing, organizing what seemed to be the impossible, and providing solutions when I could see none. Thank you to the TouchWood Editions in-house editor, Renée Layberry, for the final rounds that we went through as the book was in design and going to press. And to designer Pete Kohut for making this a beautiful object when it was merely words in my hands.

This was a book that required logistical help from perhaps too many to thank individually. However, at the risk of forgetting someone—it'll happen—I need to recognize the following key people who went out of their way as I careened up and down the valleys, madly trying to cover an area that seemed to multiply by the moment. Catherine Frechette, communications manager, and Jenny McAlpine, communications coordinator, at Tourism Kelowna; Alison Love, Spatula Media + Communications; and Ange Chew, tourism manager, Tourism Vernon—thank you for being excellent at your job. Farther afield, thanks to my agent, Chris Bucci, partner at the McDermid Agency, who cares about food and writing in equal measure, as I do. Many people contributed photos to this book, and they are noted in the photo caption credits. Dave McQueen (mcqueenphotography.ca) and Jasmin Dosanj went above and beyond. In the eleventh hour, two writer-friends, Elizabeth Withey and Claire Sear, carried me across the finish line.

Lastly, thanks, as always, to my husband, Mike, who kept our lives organized and me in touch with the wider world beyond my computer screen through this project—and for the gift of adventure that brought us to the Okanagan in the first place.

INDEX

JENNIFER COCKRALL-KING is a food culture writer and urban agriculture expert, splitting her time between Edmonton, Alberta, and the Okanagan Valley, BC. She is the author of *Food and the City: Urban Agriculture and the New Food Revolution* (Prometheus Books, 2012), which has been translated into Korean, Japanese, and French. She is also a contributor to *Integrated Urban Agriculture: Precedents, Practices, Prospects* (UBC Press, 2015).

Cockrall-King is the founder and organizer of the Okanagan Food & Wine Writers' Workshop in Kelowna (foodwinewriters.com) and a columnist and contributing editor of *Eighteen Bridges* magazine (eighteenbridges.com).

Follow her writings about food and her research trips at foodgirl.ca. You can also join her on Facebook (FoodArtisansoftheOkanagan) and on Twitter @jennifer_ck and @foodwinewriters.